Praise for *Here...*

In his easy to read conversation[al style,...] [practical tool] to strengthen their church for lo[ng-term effectiveness...] [for a resource] that will help you capture you[r dream for your church, create a path to fulfill that] at dream, and courageously pursue the dream, *Here Today, There Tomorrow* [is what you] are looking for.

—Rev. Phil Stevenson, director of church multiplication and leadership development, Pacific Southwest District of The Wesleyan Church

Gary L. McIntosh gives us a practical and biblical nine-step blueprint for developing a long-range plan for our churches.

—Rev. Bill Easum, founder and senior consultant, 21st Century Strategies

It has been said that those who do not plan for the future, plan to fail. Gary L. McIntosh has written a book to help local churches plan for the future so they can build and construct an outreach to the lost in their community to become a healthy church to fulfill the will of God. Each chapter is organized around major aspects of the planning process. Therefore the reader can go to a chapter according to the need they have in their church. However, it would be better for the reader to work through the book chapter-by-chapter to get an overview of the planning process in the local church. Anyone dealing with the future of the local church must read this book and plan accordingly.

—Dr. Elmer L. Towns, co-founder and dean of religion, Liberty University

If you are a pastor or a lay leader in a small to mid-sized church that has hit a plateau or is declining, then Gary's book will help direct your church to a new future. It is very practical and easy to understand.

—Dr. Doug Talley, executive state pastor, Indiana Ministries of the Church of God

Your first plan for an effective ministry will include this practical, must-read focus on intentionally moving a church forward. Gary L. McIntosh has provided a great guide!

—Dr. Kent Hunter, leader, Church Doctor Ministries

Here Today, There Tomorrow provides pastors and church leaders with perceptive, practical, positive assistance to produce faith-based plans that will help keep churches relevant not only today, but also tomorrow.

—Dr. Tom Steffen, professor of intercultural studies, Biola University

This is one of the finest books I have read on the subject of developing a master plan for a local church. This book is the equivalent of a seminary course in planning. Each chapter contains outstanding ideas and practical ways to develop and implement strategies to make your church meet the challenge not only of today but also of our constantly changing culture. This is a book that I believe will be widely used through churches that desire to grow and expand to the glory of God.

—Rev. Stephen Babby, district superintendent, Pacific Southwest District of The Wesleyan Church

In this very readable book, Gary L. McIntosh has addressed some essential topics (mission, vision, values, and goals) for those who wish to exercise good leadership in the local church during an era of rapid change. His topics have been addressed before, usually in multiple volumes, but this book provides an up-to-date review of these important issues in a succinct and relevant way. I found his explanations and applications to be totally consistent with local church life and needs as I know them. I would recommend this book for new pastors who might discuss the topics with an experienced mentor, and for seasoned pastors who might benefit by being reminded and reenergized on these important concepts of local church leadership.

—Dr. Kenneth E. Bickel, director and Professor of pastoral studies,
Grace Theological Seminary

Dr. McIntosh has done it again. He has provided pastors, leaders, and the Church at large with a wonderful template on how to stay relevant in the presentation of the Gospel. This book will be of great value in helping plan, coordinate, and focus their ministry for maximum effectiveness. Bravo, Gary! You have done it again.

—Dr. Chuck Lawless, dean, Billy Graham School,
Southern Seminary and president, The Lawless Group

He has written a good primer on missional leadership uniting effective evangelism with congregational vitality.

—Dr. Lyle Pointer, pastor, congregational consultant,
and former professor of evangelism, Nazarene Theological Seminary

Everything Gary writes is "Real Church Ministry Friendly." This latest book, *Here Today, There Tomorrow: Unleashing Your Church's Potential* is rooted in Scripture, rigorously tested by research and realized in local church ministry. Words of description include: *wise, clear, helpful, practical, biblical common sense, conversational,* and *motivating.* This book is a remarkable synthesis of a biblical theology of planning and best practices for local church planning that will result in genuine increased kingdom effectiveness. A major bonus is how these chapters will serve as a tool to translate the life vocational skills and gifts of lay leadership into actual ministry reality. Any church at any size, stage, or shape will profit for the sake of the Gospel by working the steps and process of this superior planning pathway.

—Dr. Dennis Baker, senior ministry consultant, The Goehner Group

HERE TODAY,
THERE TOMORROW

HERE TODAY, THERE TOMORROW

Unleashing Your Church's Potential

Gary L. McIntosh

wesleyan
publishing
house

Indianapolis, Indiana

Copyright © 2010 by Gary L. McIntosh
Published by Wesleyan Publishing House
Indianapolis, Indiana 46250
Printed in the United States of America
ISBN: 978-0-89827-422-6

Library of Congress Cataloging-in-Publication Data

McIntosh, Gary, 1947-
Here today, there tomorrow : unleashing your church's potential / Gary L. McIntosh.
    p. cm.
ISBN 978-0-89827-422-6
1. Church. 2. Change--Religious aspects--Christianity. I. Title.
BV600.3.M3535 2010
254'.6--dc22
                                    2009041243

To Lyle E. Schaller,
author, consultant, and guide,
for your insightful understanding of the local church.

Contents

Acknowledgements

M uch thanks to the following persons who helped make this book possible. First, my research assistant at Talbot School of Theology, Katie Dudgeon, for her help in researching material on the biblical basis of planning. Second, my personal editor, Laura McIntosh, who makes me look like a better writer that I am. Third, to the fine folks at Wesleyan Publishing House—Don Cady, Craig Bubeck, Kevin Scott, Rachael Stevenson, and Joe Jackson—for their dedicated work in bringing this book to publication. I appreciate all of you.

If you fail to plan, you are planning to fail.
—AUTHOR UNKNOWN

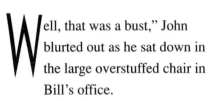

ONE

Get on Board

W ell, that was a bust," John blurted out as he sat down in the large overstuffed chair in Bill's office.

"Slow down a bit," Bill motioned with the palm of his right hand toward John. "What's the story behind that comment?"

"Sorry to begin so bluntly," John quickly apologized, "but I'm so frustrated from last night's board meeting that I don't know what to do. Thanks for taking time to meet with me this morning. I just need someone to talk to."

"No problem, John. You know I'm always available to help," Bill smiled.

"I'm just frustrated that our church isn't moving forward," John continued with a bit of nervous energy in his voice. "There are plenty of opportunities to engage our community with the love of Christ, but my church is so tangled up in itself, we can't take advantage of them."

"It sounds like you have a vision for the church that the leaders don't understand or aren't embracing. Am I right?" Bill asked pointedly.

"No, I'd say we have too many visions," John rejoined. "We have too many dreams."

"Too many dreams? I don't get it," Bill reflected with curiosity.

"What I mean is some people think we should be a witness for Christ, others think we ought to serve humanity, and still others feel our purpose is to care for the needy. The problem is that none of these grand themes are clearly defined. Every year we do the same things without thinking about what God is doing in our community."

"I see what you mean," Bill agreed. "Does your church have a long-range plan?"

"Long-range plan?" John laughed. "We tried to develop a plan a few years ago, but we spent so much time planning that we never actually did anything. Talk about frustration. Wow!"

"That may be true," Bill retorted, "but someone once said, 'If you fail to plan, you are planning to fail.'"

"Yes, I agree. But how does a church develop a plan that actually works?" John asked.

Three Challenges

This conversation illustrates three aspects of church ministry that challenge all leaders.

First, churches tend to function day-to-day, week-to-week, month-to-month, and year-to-year doing pretty much the same things. They assume that existing ministries continue to be sufficient for today's needs and tomorrow's opportunities. Thus, churches tend to keep doing what they have always done, and, of course, they keep getting the results they have always had.

Second, churches often try to do too much. There are so many good things a church can do—and perhaps should do—that many tie themselves in proverbial knots doing very little. Witnessing, caring, loving, serving, worshiping, and teaching are all part of a church's role. However, where does a church start? What are its priorities? Where does it invest its limited resources? What should it leave undone? Church leaders who are unable to answer these kinds of questions often remain frustrated, and their churches accomplish little.

Third, church leaders instinctively know that designing a plan and working from a set of clear goals is important to fruitfulness. Yet, they wonder how best to plan, particularly in a world where change happens so quickly that plans seem out of date before they are put into action.

Down in the Mud

Churches are often prone to what Ed Dayton and Ted Engstrom called *down in the mud* disease. While leaders of World Vision International, Dayton and Engstrom discovered churches tend to get bogged down when a large number of committees, departments, or boards "are organized around *what* they do rather than what task they are trying to complete." They point out:

> In the local church this might show itself in a multiplying number of Boards of Christian Education, Visitation Committees, Ushering Committees, Building Committees, etc. When these groups are formed, they usually have a clear idea of why and what. But after ten years, their original goals become fuzzy, and institutional hardening of the arteries sets in. Each year new budgets are approved which are just an extension of "What we did last year."[1]

Over time, this tendency to replicate what has always been done results in a church that is bogged down in the mud. Unfortunately, the best reports on the state of the church say 80 to 85 percent of churches are running in mud. Some—no one knows exactly how many—are stuck in the mud. Taking steps forward is difficult, even with the best of intentions, but running in mud is impossible.

So, how do churches stuck in the mud get moving again? To begin, a church must define its basic purpose, determine the goals that will fulfill that purpose, and align its resources in a way that will empower the accomplishment of its goals.

This sounds good in theory, but it is difficult to do. As one insightful person once pointed out, "In theory, there is no difference between theory and practice, but in practice there is."

The old saying, "If you fail to plan, you are planning to fail," is true. Yet, how does a church go about developing a plan that works? That is the purpose of *Here Today, There Tomorrow*—to provide a simple but effective way to plan the future of your church and unleash its full potential.

Planning and the Will of God

Planning is our attempt to understand the will of God for our church and respond to it by our actions. A leader once put it this way, "We must find out what God is doing and get on board." Designing a plan is not about discovering what we want for our church, but about what God wants for our church. God is working in our church and community right now. Our job is to discover what he is blessing and mold our church to fit his plans.

What God is blessing or doing is his will, but we have to respond. By choosing a course of action for the future, we respond to what God is already doing. Our plans do not have to identify every single step in the future of the church. Indeed we cannot really know all the steps

God wants us to take. But by imagining the future of our church through developing a plan, we start moving in the direction God points, trusting him to fill in the details as we move forward.

All congregations are involved in planning, whether or not they call it that. Someone makes decisions about the allocation of financial resources; determines how to use the church building and grounds; sets the schedule for worship; organizes programs for children; assigns volunteers to various ministries; and designates priorities for witness, missions, and social action. However, few churches design a comprehensive plan that brings the entire efforts of the church to focus on a common mission and vision that aligns with their understanding of the will of God. Churches are most likely to have such a comprehensive plan when they are a new church plant or when they are constructing new facilities. In both of these instances, having a comprehensive master plan helps to insure that the church's overall vision enjoys full support from all the people. While it is important to make daily plans in all areas of church life and ministry, it is the development of a coherent, coordinated, and unifying comprehensive master plan to which *Here Today, There Tomorrow* speaks.

What to Expect

Each chapter of *Here Today, There Tomorrow* is organized to address a major question or aspect about the planning process. Glance over the contents and, if you see a chapter that interests you or addresses a question or need you are currently facing, feel free to turn to that chapter and begin reading there.

However, if the concept of constructing a comprehensive plan is new to you, I recommend working through this book chapter by chapter to gain a thorough overview of the planning process in a local church.

As you will discover, chapters 2 through 9 relate to foundational issues. These chapters provide valuable groundwork for understanding how to develop a master plan in a local church. Since developing a plan starts with a clear understanding that planning is biblical, chapter 2 places us on solid ground by discussing the biblical foundations for planning. It points out how God himself is a planner.

If you want a simple overview of the planning cycle as found in most churches, jump ahead to chapter 3. The planning in most churches follows a defined process. There is no need for churches to clear a new pathway; most can follow the beaten path other churches have created.

The five essential principles that undergird planning are outlined in chapter 4, and chapter 5 details how to assemble an effective planning team.

Taking inventory of the current state of the church is a necessary prerequisite to building a solid plan for the future. Chapter 6 presents several ways to evaluate the fruitfulness of your church's ministries. Taking an honest look at what is happening in your church is a must before beginning the planning process.

Since new people are most often reached through new ministries, chapter 7 focuses on designing programs that reach out to new people. Generating new ideas for ministry is a challenge in most churches, and chapter 8 presents ideas to freshen up your church through new innovative plans. Of course, new ideas lead to change. So, chapter 9 offers insight on initiating change in a church.

Are you ready to move forward quickly on the actual plan itself? Begin reading with chapter 10 and continue through chapter 14; these chapters spell out the main components found in an effective plan. For example, we talk in depth in these chapters about how to understand and develop a church's mission, values, vision, and goals. Chapter 15 concludes with a final survey of how planning helps build a solid church ministry. A sample plan from a real church is included in appendix B.

An additional feature in this book is "My Planning Notebook." At the end of each chapter, the essential ideas, insights, and principles are listed in an outline form. If you are busy or just want a quick peek at what each chapter includes, start with "My Planning Notebook" for each chapter. There is space to add your own thoughts to the notebook as you read through this book.

There is a story of an airline pilot who announced over the intercom system, "Ladies and gentlemen, I have good news and bad news. The good news is that we have a tailwind, and we are making excellent time. The bad news is that our compass is broken, and we have no idea where we are going." Your church is running a lot of programs, but is it doing the right things? Your church leaders are putting out a lot of fires, but are they doing the essential things? Your church is making excellent time, but is it going anywhere? To find out where your church is in this regard, ask yourself the following questions:

1. Does our church have a written plan of ministry?
2. If we asked our people, "What is our church's purpose?" would we get a consistent answer?
3. Have we talked about our church's purpose from the pulpit in the last three months? In adult classes or groups? In private conversation?
4. Have recent church decisions been directly influenced by our purpose?
5. Is there cooperation among various ministry areas in our church? Does each ministry area know where it fits in the total direction of the church?

If your answer to many of these questions is no, you can be sure you need a master plan for your congregation.

Where is your church right now? Are you ready to begin developing a plan so you can be here today and there tomorrow? Then let's get started by considering the biblical foundation for planning.

MY PLANNING NOTEBOOK

Beginning Insights:

- If we fail to plan, we are planning to fail.

My Comments:

- Definition: Planning is our attempt to understand the will of God for our church and respond to it by our actions.

My Comments:

- We must find out what God is doing and get on board.

My Comments:

NOTE

1. Ted Engstrom and Ed Dayton, "How to Get Where You're Going," *Christian Leadership Letter* (Monrovia, Calif.: World Vision, August 1987), 1–2.

The mind of man plans his way,
But the LORD directs his steps.
—PROVERBS 16:9

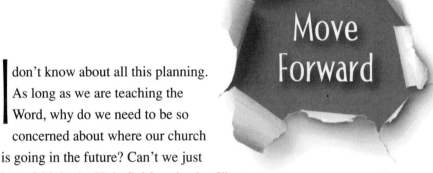

TWO

Move Forward

I don't know about all this planning. As long as we are teaching the Word, why do we need to be so concerned about where our church is going in the future? Can't we just have faith in the Holy Spirit to lead us?"

Long-term planning in the church today is just like corporate planning—church leaders may have good intentions, but their strategic planning has strategized the Holy Spirit right out of church ministry.

Somewhere deep inside many churches there is a sense that planning is not biblical—that those who really trust the Lord will accomplish things in a more spiritual way. They believe that too much planning for the future leaves God out of the picture and rests entirely on human strength and insight. Others assert that strategic planning is a corporate concept that churches have thoughtlessly borrowed from the business world. These conclusions are born out of a poor understanding of what planning really is.

A Biblical Perspective on Planning

Planning is no more than an attempt to understand the will of God for our church and respond to it by our actions. It is not an independent humanistic activity that thwarts God's ability to work. It can be a spiritual activity that is an expression of our faith in God. Sensing where the Lord is leading and making a unified effort to move in that direction actually honors God and displays our trust in him. Planning is not a faithless activity or a trendy technique stolen from corporate America—it is what believers do as faithful stewards of God's resources. Thinking of planning in this light, we see it emerge as a key theme throughout Scripture.

Planning as Wisdom

Planning and giving forethought to decisions is described as wise behavior throughout the book of Proverbs. Those who plan seek guidance and give forethought to their future are considered wise and held in contrast with those who do not. Proverbs 13:16 says, "A wise man thinks ahead; a fool doesn't, and even brags about it!" (TLB). Proverbs 14:15 adds, "A simple man believes anything, but a prudent man gives thought to his steps" (NIV). Those who do not think about their future are considered foolish, while those who plan and spend time seeking the Lord's direction are wise and prudent. Additionally, Proverbs suggests that those who make hasty decisions make poor, uninformed decisions (19:2), while those who seek the Lord together and commit their plans to him will experience success (15:22; 16:3).

Paul, in 1 Corinthians, explains his behavior in light of these principles. Even though his ministry plans changed, he wanted the Corinthians to know that it was not on account of carelessness or a lack of planning. He had significant spiritual reasons for postponing his visit to them. He felt the need, as a minister of the gospel committed to their spiritual growth, to explain his rationale for the change in plans.

Planning as Good Stewardship

Not only is planning a wise activity with great benefit, it makes possible good stewardship of the resources God entrusts to us. As church leaders, we are responsible to handle the resources of the church in a way that furthers God's kingdom; this is only possible when we take time to plan. Good stewardship is more than spending a budget wisely; it includes using the resources God gives us to minister to others in an intentional way. We want our churches to move forward in a way that honors God, honors the resources he has given us, and honors the opportunities he places before us. When we are short sighted or fail to recognize the long-term significance of the decisions we are making, we miss opportunities to be faithful and fruitful for the future.

In Acts 6, Luke describes a growing church that was missing opportunities to minister because it was disorganized. The Holy Spirit was transforming lives, and the church was bursting at the seams with new believers. But there was a problem. A growing number of widows in Jerusalem were going without food and being overlooked in the distribution of resources to help them. The issue was finally brought to the attention of the leaders, and they put a plan in place to solve the problem.

Even though this new church had the people and material resources needed to care for the widows, they were ineffective in responding to the needs, because they did not have a plan. They had not taken time to set priorities, delegate responsibilities, and coordinate tasks. Like the church of Acts 6, when we fail to plan, we fail to be good stewards of the opportunities God gives us to meet needs and minister to those around us.

Planning as Faith

Scripture is clear that God is the one who develops plans and brings fruit through our plans; in this way our planning is an expression of our faith in him. We try to listen and discern his voice as we plan, but biblical planning also recognizes the role of God to empower the plans. Proverbs 16:9 says that, "The heart of man plans his way, but the LORD establishes his steps" (ESV). Although we make plans and work hard to accomplish them, ultimately we trust in the Lord to bring success and spiritual progress.

> Planning is an expression of our faith in God.

Paul recognized the unique role God plays in advancing or prospering ministry: "I planted, Apollos watered, but God gave the growth" (1 Cor. 3:6 NRSV). True spiritual change and growth comes from the Lord, and our long-term planning honors the vital role that the Lord plays in the realization of any goals.

Planning is also an expression of our faith—we are putting our confidence in the Lord, expecting him to work. We can plan confidently because God is faithful and we know his purposes will be accomplished. Proverbs 19:21 says that, "Many are the plans in the mind of a man, but it is the purpose of the LORD that will stand" (ESV). We may not know exactly how our needs or goals will be met—especially in the initial stages of planning—but we move forward, trusting in his guidance and provision. Even if our plans do not entirely align with God's purposes, planning is not futile. We can plan confidently because we know his purposes will ultimately prevail.

God may sometimes alter our plans to accomplish his purposes, but this does not diminish the significance or value of seeking him and developing a plan. This point is illustrated in Acts 16, where Paul and his companions plan to preach and minister in Asia. When they attempted to go to Asia, the Spirit of Jesus did not allow them to enter Bithynia and minister there. Instead, they were directed in a vision to go to Macedonia. Wisely, they decided to change course so they could minister where God wanted them, despite their previous plans.

It is interesting to note that Paul and his companions were not in the wrong for having a plan, nor were they reprimanded for attempting to accomplish a plan different than what God wanted. However, they were open to a change in their plan and willingly responded to it after concluding that the Lord wanted them to minister in Macedonia instead of Asia. There are times when God's plans will trump our plans, but that does not diminish the value of planning.

> Planning allows us to be good stewards of the
> opportunities God brings to our church.

Planning is not, then, something reserved for corporations or something that is unspiritual. It is a wise activity that allows us to be good stewards of the opportunities for ministry that God brings our way. And when we plan, we are expressing our faith and confidence in the Lord.

God the Planner

Planning is central to accomplishing God's purposes in Scripture, and three examples from Scripture affirm the significance of planning. First, God himself plans and interacts with humanity based on his good plans and purposes for humanity. Second, the necessity and significance of planning can be seen in the building of the tabernacle in Exodus. Third, God uses the plans and leadership of his servants to accomplish specific tasks, like when Nehemiah rebuilt the wall in Jerusalem.

God was deliberate about the way he created the world and the order in which he created things. There is a logic and progression to the seven days of creation described in Genesis 1–2, which reveal his thoughtfulness and intentionality. He has the power and the authority to do what he pleases when he pleases, yet he deliberately chose to create the world with forethought, order, and systems.

God carefully developed complex and intricate systems that allow humanity to coexist and interact with nature. This is reflected in Genesis 1:

> God blessed [Adam and Eve] and said to them, "Be fruitful and increase in number; fill the earth and subdue it. Rule over the fish of the sea and the birds of the air and over every living creature that moves on the ground."
>
> Then God said, "I give you every seed-bearing plant on the face of the whole earth and every tree that has fruit with seed in it. They will be yours for food. And to all the beasts of the earth and all the birds of the air and all the creatures that move on the ground—everything that has the breath of life in it—I give every green plant for food." And it was so. (Gen. 1:28–30 NIV)

God designed the world to operate in a specific way to provide for and bless humanity, and the instructions he gave Adam and Eve reflect his plan for the created order.

God also knew, from the beginning of time, that sin would destroy his relationship with people and that he would need to provide a solution to the sin problem. Although Christ did not come to earth as a man until the first century, he was part of God's plan and existed with God at creation. In reference to Christ, John 1:1–2 says, "In the beginning was the Word, and the Word was with God, and the Word was God. He was with God in the beginning" (NIV). Christ existed before creation and was part of God's plan to redeem humanity. The profundity of God's activity is highlighted for us in Ephesians 1:4 when Paul says, "For he chose us in him before the creation of the world to be holy and blameless in his sight" (NIV).

The Old Testament is the story of God working to redeem his people, reveal his gracious plan for them, and prepare them to receive Christ as Savior. Before Adam and Eve were even able to begin grasping the depth of the consequences of their choices, he began revealing his solution—or plan of redemption—to them. After the fall in Genesis 3, the Lord says to the serpent, "I will put enmity between you and the woman, and between your offspring and hers; he will crush your head, and you will strike his heel" (v. 15 NIV). The Lord is recognizing the spiritual battle that will ensue because of the power of sin, but he offers hope in the offspring of Eve who will have victory over Satan. Christ fulfilled this promise, demonstrating that God was prepared to address the sin problem through the person and work of Christ even in Genesis.

God is not haphazard, casual, or unintentional about addressing the sin problem of humanity, nor does he approach the Christian life that way. God is intentional about calling his people to serve him and equipping them to do so. Ephesians 2:10 says, "For we are His workmanship, created in Christ Jesus for good works, which God prepared beforehand so that we would walk in them." God has already prepared opportunities and placed circumstances in our lives to serve; our responsibility is simply to accept them. Believers do not have to orchestrate opportunities for themselves or desperately search for some way to serve and live out the Christian life. God has already done the work and prepared opportunities for us in advance. God's work is characterized by planning, and it is through his plans for creation, redemption, and service that we see how integral planning is to achieving his good purposes in our individual and corporate lives.

> Planning characterizes the way God works
> in creation, redemption, and service.

The value God places on planning is also reflected in the process he prescribed for building the tabernacle. The instructions and specifications for the tabernacle in Exodus 25–40 provide a great example of the importance of planning. These chapters are filled with detailed descriptions on such things like the color and pattern of the curtains, the measurements of certain beams, the type of wood to be used, and the exact items that are to be inside the tabernacle. Why is there such great detail about the building of the tabernacle in these passages? What does this tell us about planning and the significance of the tabernacle?

The detailed descriptions and specifications given to Moses in Exodus reflect the significance of the tabernacle as God's dwelling place. Building the tabernacle was not just a worthwhile endeavor; it was the best investment God's people could make with their time and energy. The tabernacle was so special that it required a detailed plan to ensure its proper completion.

The same is true for ministry today. God has given us wonderful opportunities that are worth the investment of our time and energy. Although we may not be building a literal tabernacle, he has given us opportunities and ministries that deserve our attention and care. When we commit the time and energy to plan, we are recognizing the spiritual value of these opportunities and honoring the ministry God has entrusted to us.

Nehemiah: Master Planner

Nehemiah is an example of a leader who planned well, led diligently, and successfully completed the task God gave him. Nehemiah was in a great position of influence as cupbearer to the king, and he used this position wisely to accomplish great things for the city of Jerusalem. When he learned about the poor state of the walls and gates of Jerusalem after the Babylonian exile, God laid it upon his heart to lead the rebuilding process. He did not rush into the task and begin the rebuilding process hastily. Instead, he sought the Lord's guidance and direction from the moment his heart was stirred. He approached the king with his requests only after approaching the Lord in prayer.

Nehemiah was intentional in the way he approached the king. His requests were specific and his decisions were wise because he spent time observing, gathering information, and calculating what it would take to rebuild the walls. He was intentional about developing a plan to rebuild the wall—acquiring the necessary resources, delegating and utilizing the skills of others, and remaining focused amidst great opposition. Nehemiah did not act independently of God, but rather Nehemiah's skills and plans provided the vehicle for God to accomplish his purposes for Jerusalem.

After the completion of the wall, Nehemiah asked the Lord to honor his hard work. "Remember me for this, O my God, and do not blot out what I have so faithfully done for the house of my God and its services" (Neh. 13:14 NIV). Nehemiah faithfully served the Lord through planning and intentional leadership, and the Lord blessed the commitment and diligence he showed in the rebuilding process.

Whether it is through God's plan for creation, redemption, or good works, we see in Scripture that God is a planner. God brings about his good purposes for us through his plans. Any activity or task of significance, such as building the tabernacle or rebuilding the wall in Jerusalem, is worthy of a comprehensive plan to ensure its completion. Planning reflects an aspect of God's character as well as the spiritual value of the tasks at hand.

PLANNING FROM PROVERBS (TLB)

FACTS

"You simpletons!" she cries. "How long will you go on being fools? How long will you scoff at wisdom and fight the facts? Come here and listen to me! I'll pour out the spirit of wisdom upon you, and make you wise."

"For you closed your eyes to the facts and did not choose to reverence and trust the Lord, and you turned your back on me, spurning my advice" (1:22–23, 29–30).

PLAN AHEAD

"A wise man thinks ahead; a fool doesn't and even brags about it!" (13:16).

RELIABLE INFORMATION

"An unreliable messenger can cause a lot of trouble. Reliable communication permits progress" (13:17).

PLANNING

"It is pleasant to see plans develop. That is why fools refuse to give them up even when they are wrong" (13:19).

PLANNING AND ADVICE

"Plans go wrong with too few counselors; many counselors bring success" (15:22).

PLANNING AND GOD'S PART

"We can make our plans, but the final outcome is in God's Hands" (16:1).

PLANNING AND GOD

"We should make plans—counting on God to direct us" (16:9).

DECISION MAKING AND THE FACTS

"What a shame—yes, how stupid!—to decide before knowing the facts!" (18:13).

NEW IDEAS: ACCEPT OR RESIST?

"The intelligent man is always open to new ideas. In fact, he looks for them" (18:15).

ACTION WITHOUT INFORMATION

"It is dangerous and sinful to rush into the unknown" (19:2).

PLANNING AND THE ADVICE OF OTHERS

"Don't go ahead with your plans without the advice of others; don't go to war until they agree" (20:18).

PROJECTING AHEAD

"A prudent man foresees the difficulties ahead and prepares for them; the simpleton goes blindly on and suffers the consequences" (22:3).

PLANNING, COMMON SENSE, AND KEEPING ABREAST OF THE FACTS

"Any enterprise is built by wise planning, becomes strong through common sense, and profits wonderfully by keeping abreast of the facts" (24:3–4).

PLANNING AND PUBLIC RELATIONS

"Don't brag about your plans for tomorrow—wait and see what happens" (27:1).

MY PLANNING NOTEBOOK

Biblical Planning

- Planning is an expression of our faith in God.

My Comments:

- Planning allows us to be good stewards of the opportunities God brings to our church.

My Comments:

- Planning characterizes the way God works in creation, redemption, and service.

My Comments:

It is possible to spend more time planning than the fruits of our planning will warrant.

—Author Unknown

THREE

On the Beaten Path

When I first started consulting with churches, *long-range* meant developing a five to ten year plan. In our fast changing world today, long-range is more like two to three years. Even though the planning cycle for most churches does not extend as far into the future as it once did, it is still important that churches plan for the future.

There are several types of plans that church leaders make on a regular basis. First, there are *standing plans*, sometimes called policies. Standing plans assist churches to handle (a) issues that come up frequently, such as weddings, baptisms, and use of facilities; (b) emergency situations, such as what to do in case of a fire or if someone is injured on the church campus; and (c) unexpected situations, such as when a decision must be made but those with authority to make decisions are not available.

> There are three types of plans: standing plans,
> routine plans, and new plans.

A second type of planning results in *routine plans*, sometimes called schedules. Routine planning predicts what will take place on a daily, a weekly, a monthly, or a yearly time frame. Churches typically operate with master calendars for worship; adult, youth, and children's activities; and a host of other ministry functions that take place in a routine manner.

A third type of planning is to develop *new plans*. This form of planning goes by several names—master planning, long-range planning, or simply planning ahead. This third type of planning is the focus of *Here Today, There Tomorrow*. Failure to do this type of planning can cause ordinary problems to become emergency problems.

An Overview of the Planning Process

At this point, it may be helpful to take a bird's-eye view of the overall planning process. The next chapters will focus on individual aspects of planning, but the entire process progresses along a nine-step format.

Step One: Establish a Mission

The first step in the planning cycle is for a church to determine its reason for being. This is where a church searches Scripture to find out what God wants the church to do. It is the biblical reason the church exists.

Many churches have a mission statement on the books that is not widely known or used by people in the church today. Every generation of the church must rethink its mission for itself. This is a natural aspect of life as generations succeed one another. Mission must be reconceptualized in new phrases, so that it communicates to new generations in ways that excite them for the future of their church.

A church I visited a few years ago has its mission statement inscribed in the concrete walkway in front of the church. It reads, "To Know Christ and To Make Him Known." The statement is a biblical way to understand the church's mission. Unfortunately, the phrase was popular nearly one hundred years ago and has now been around so long that it seems old. While the statement is biblical, it has little power to inspire a new generation of believers. This church and many others must find a new statement of mission if they hope to restore lost vitality.

Step Two: Establish a Vision

After a fresh restatement of the mission, leaders must then craft a compelling statement of how big an impact God wants their church to make in the world. Where will the church focus its efforts, and how wide and deep of an impact does the church wish to make on the community, nation, and world?

A vision provides specificity regarding how a church will fulfill its mission, so that people are emotionally energized to give, to serve, and to participate in order to empower its fulfillment. While churches often have a mission statement, few have taken time to design a powerful vision that moves a church forward.

Step Three: Establish Core Values

The essential morals, principles, or ideals that support the overall church ministry are the congregation's core values. Values are what a church holds on to no matter what happens. They are nonnegotiable convictions that shape how the mission and vision of the church will be fulfilled. Every church operates by its own values system, even if they do not realize it. Taking time to identify and note the active values that drive a church's ministry is an important step in designing a comprehensive plan for the future.

Step Four: Establish Strategy

Strategy is a step-by-step description of how a church hopes to accomplish its vision. Church leaders evaluate the church's ministry context, resources, obstacles, demographics, and needs—both internally and externally. Out of such evaluation comes the ministry design (strategy) to fulfill the overarching vision. A strategy is typically designed and communicated as a series of *objectives*—major initiatives that the congregation is committed to accomplishing.

Step Five: Establish Goals

Goals are measurable, attainable, track-able statements of what is to be accomplished. For example, "train six new greeters by November first" or "purchase a new projector by May fifteenth" are examples of goals. Each can be measured and tracked to see whether or not they are actually done. To be effective, an objective must be broken down into several smaller, achievable goals. Thus, if a church achieves all its goals, it can be assumed it will also fulfill its objectives.

Step Six: Establish Action Plans

Action plans are detailed statements of when something will be accomplished and who will accomplish it. They always include target dates for completion and the names of specific people who will do the work. Action plans must never be delegated to a committee, as there needs to be a specific individual who is accountable.

Step Seven: Align Resources

For plans to be accomplished, resources need to be allocated for them. Aligning people, money, prayer, and facility resources to support each and every goal ensures the likelihood it will be accomplished. If too few resources are allocated, the potential for failure increases.

Step Eight: Implement Plans

Of the nine steps, this is the most difficult one to accomplish. Many church leaders find the planning process to be thrilling, while actually executing the plan is a different story. My experience assisting churches to implement plans has convinced me that the first year of creating plans and beginning to implement them is the easiest. The second year of working through the difficulties and challenges brought on by the plan is the most difficult. The third year is where the fruit is harvested. The bottom line is a plan must be worked for at least three years if a church wants to see results.

> To stay fit, churches must develop a new plan
> every three to five years.

Step Nine: Adjust Plans

No plan is perfect, and even the best of plans will encounter difficulties. Whether something was overlooked in the original plan, unexpected challenges arise, crises occur, or leaders relocate out of town, rarely is a plan fully implemented as it was originally conceived. This means a long-range plan must be monitored, audited, and adjusted each step of the way. After two to three years, the planning cycle begins anew.

Recycle the Planning Cycle

Recycling the planning process is especially important, since churches follow a predictable life cycle very similar to that of a human life cycle. As the chart below demonstrates, humans go through at least nine stages of development from birth to young adult to eventual death.

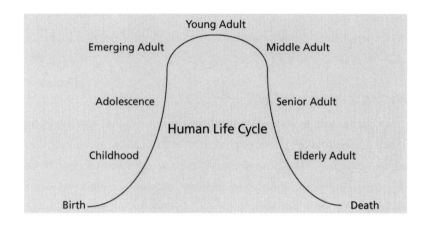

A Church's Typical Life Cycle

What most people in our churches do not realize is that there is also a typical life cycle for churches.[1] By changing the words on the illustration above, we can show the common congregational life cycle found in churches. As the second chart shows, churches go through a predictable cycle of birth and growth, followed by a period of plateau, and then eventual decline and death.

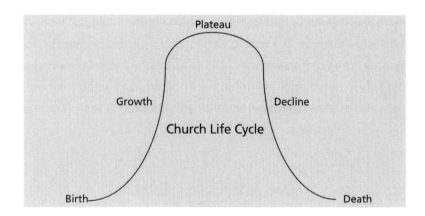

When the birth of a church takes place, there is often a feeling of excitement and hope for the future. This enthusiasm propels the church to experience growth over the next three to five years. In fact, this early vision of the future may even carry a church for ten to twenty years or more, depending on the expanse of the vision. It is sort of like tracking your children through childhood, adolescence, and into college.

Eventually a church moves onto a plateau, which may last from twenty to sixty years. A lot of good ministry takes place during this time of plateau. Missionaries are sent to the field, people are won to Christ, and children are discipled. But ever so slowly, the church experiences more plateau and less growth. A way to observe the typical life cycle of a church is found in the drawing below.

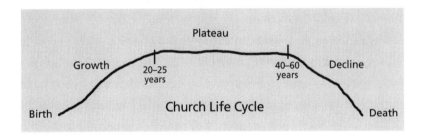

The growth phase of a church normally lasts about twenty to twenty-five years. While there are exceptions, the best years of growth for most churches are over by their twenty-fifth birthday. The remaining years are not necessarily bad ones, but there is a slowing of growth as the church moves into a maintenance mode of ministry. Unfortunately, if this leveling off is not challenged, the result is the inevitable decline and eventual death of the church.

A church dies when it closes its doors or when it becomes so ineffective that it no longer carries out the Great Commission. No one really knows for sure, but the best estimates are that about four thousand churches close their doors every year.[2] Many others remain open, even though they are not effectively fulfilling their purpose.

It reminds me of the story about a young boy who went fishing with his grandfather. As they walked from their car to the lake, they happened upon a small turtle. Immediately the grandfather took out his pocketknife and cut off the turtle's head to use as bait. After fishing for a short while, the boy and his grandfather walked back to the car to eat their picnic lunch. As they walked by the turtle's body, the boy noticed it was still moving. "Grandpa!" he exclaimed. "That turtle is still alive!"

His grandfather replied, "No, he's dead. He just doesn't know it yet." Like that turtle, many churches are so ineffective they are dead; they just do not realize it yet.[3]

The church life cycle I have described is so predictable it has been named St. John's Syndrome.[4] The name comes from the last book of the Bible: Revelation. As you may recall, St. John received a vision while he was exiled on the island of Patmos. In the first part of his vision, he saw seven stars representing seven churches. The angel in John's vision instructed him to write letters to each of the churches. Each church had started out well but gradually became less effective as it grew older. St. John's Syndrome is the tendency of churches to become less effective the longer they are in existence. I call this the life cycle of a church without intervention.

Escaping the Cycle

The good news is that a local congregation does not have to follow the typical life cycle. It can be changed. Churches do not need to blindly travel this path. They can take action to restore the vitality they once experienced.

The main reason churches begin to plateau and eventually decline as they move through their life cycle is that they lose a sense of vision. As a church fulfills and moves beyond its initial vision, it faces a natural point where it will either renew its vision for the future or begin a slow decline leading along the normal life cycle. If a new vision is captured, communicated, and supported, the church most often moves forward in a new spurt of growth. When a church fails to develop a new vision, it most often begins a slow movement toward decline (see figure below).

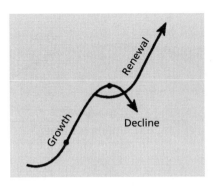

No matter where your church is on its natural life cycle,
it can start a fresh cycle.

Consider how a church's vision is developed, fulfilled, and then sometimes forgotten as it moves along its life cycle. When a church is birthed, it has a very clear vision. A church planter may have a dream to establish a work for God in a specific location. As this vision is shared with others, a team of highly committed individuals bands together and eventually gives birth to the dream as a church is established. During the next five to ten years, the church purchases its first property and builds its initial facilities. New ministries are established that reach people for Christ, and newcomers are easily connected to the growing body of believers. By the time the church is twenty to twenty-five years old, the founding members look back with pride at what has been accomplished. Their initial vision has been accomplished, and they exhale a well-deserved breath of satisfaction for a job well done. Unfortunately, the great majority of churches move onto a plateau, which over time becomes a decline, in part because the original vision was never replaced. Eventually the members say, "I remember when . . ." as they look backward to better days when the church had a clear vision that inspired commitment and involvement.

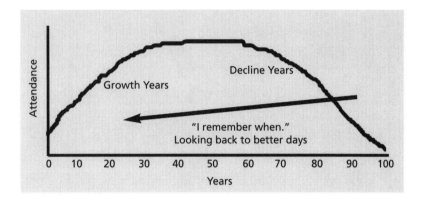

If a church desires to remain healthy over many years, it must develop a new vision. Thus, one of the most effective ways to keep a church going and growing with a continuous sense of vision is to complete a comprehensive plan every three to five years. Working through the planning cycle every two or three years keeps a church focused on what it should be doing and empowers it to stop what it should not be doing (see figure below).

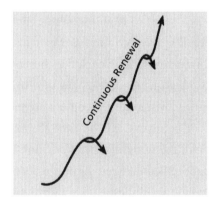

No matter where your church finds itself on its natural life cycle, it is not too late to restore your church's vision and create a new cycle of vitality. The fact that you are reading this book points to the potential for renewal. So keep reading and apply what you discover by starting a planning process in your church.

MY PLANNING NOTEBOOK

Planning Cycles:

- Churches use three types of plans: standing plans, routine plans, and new plans.

My Comments:

- To stay fit, churches must develop a new plan every three to five years.

My Comments:

- No matter where our church is on the natural life cycle, we can begin a new cycle.

NOTES

1. For a full discussion of the life cycle of a church, see my book: *Taking Your Church to the Next Level* (Grand Rapids, Mich.: Baker Books, 2009).

2. For supportive research for this number of closings, see Kevin D. Dougherty, Jared Maier, and Brian Vander Lugt, "When the Final Bell Tolls: Patterns of Church Closings in Two Protestant Denominations," an unpublished paper presented at the Michigan Academy of Science, Arts, and Letters, Ypsilanti, Mich., 2005.

3. For insights on when to close a church, see Stephen Gray and Franklin Dumond, *Legacy Churches* (St. Charles, Ill.: ChurchSmart, 2009).

4. For a full discussion of St. John's Syndrome, see C. Peter Wagner, *Your Church Can Be Healthy* (Nashville, Tenn.: Abingdon, 1979).

An intelligent plan is the first step to success.
Planning is the open road to your destination.
If you don't know where you are going, how
can you expect to get there?

—Basil S. Walsh

FOUR

Take Five

I t was a beautiful design. God clearly wanted it done. But how were they going to carry it out?

God commanded his people to go into the wilderness to build a tabernacle that would serve as the center of their worship experience. It required more than a ton of gold, almost four tons of silver, and yard upon yard of the finest fabric. How could this be done? Who would do it? Where would the resources come from—in the midst of a desert?

Your vision may not be as daunting as the tabernacle God asked Moses to build in the wilderness. The challenges may not be as unnerving; indeed you may not even be building a facility. The principles that Moses used, however, are still foundational for understanding planning in our day. In this chapter, we will discuss five principles Moses used that can help us understand how to design an excellent plan for our own ministry.

The Principle of Visionary Leadership

After a half century of research into the theological principles, procedures, and methodologies for church growth, one factor has consistently risen to the surface—*visionary leadership*. It does not matter if the goal is to plant a new church, improve an existing ministry, or turn around a declining church—all studies agree that visionary leadership is a key factor for getting the job done. For example, in 1976, C. Peter Wagner reported, "Vital Sign Number One of a healthy, growing church is a pastor who is a possibility thinker and whose dynamic leadership has been used to catalyze the entire church into action for growth."[1] A more recent study conducted by Ed Stetzer and Mike Dodson reached a similar conclusion. After surveying 324 churches that reversed a decline, the authors reported, "Leadership is the most important factor in making a comeback."[2] Describing the type of leadership that is needed to turn a church around, the authors note, "Survey respondents describe an environment where the ministry is shared with the people based upon a common vision."[3]

> Leadership is the ability to see reality, envision a preferred future, and design a plan that takes people forward.

Moses was the point person—the visionary leader—who led the way for Israel to go into the wilderness and build the tabernacle. His willingness to listen to God, take a risk, and move out without knowing all the answers paved the way for the people to leave Egypt.

At its root, leadership is the ability to see the present situation of a church, envision a better future, and then develop a plan to take the people to that future. Effective planning takes place when leadership decisions are driven by a God-given vision of hope for a better future in your church.

The Principle of Investment

Moses was gone longer on the mountain than the people expected, in part because God was giving him a detailed plan of action for the tabernacle. Unfortunately, the people saw this as a waste of time, so they decided to move forward without a God-given vision for the future. Their reactionary response brought the tabernacle project to a temporary standstill.

God showed Moses that planning is an investment rather than an expenditure of time. The plan God gave to Moses reveals an extreme amount of detailed planning. God gave Moses specific instructions for everything: curtains, lamp stands, boards, sockets, screens, garments, and altars. He told Moses how to raise the money, find the workers, and consecrate the priests. It demonstrates with certainty that God moves forward by means of a plan; the inference is that we should plan well too.

The completed tabernacle was just the way God envisioned it. How did this happen? God invested in developing and communicating a plan, and the people worked the plan. "Just as the LORD had commanded, this they had done" (Ex. 39:43). The fruitfulness of any endeavor occurs in ratio to its planning. There was a solid plan for the tabernacle, detailed in every way, and it resulted in a fine finished product.

The Principle of Goal Ownership

A wise leader summarized the principle of goal ownership this way: "My plans are good plans; your plans are bad plans." Effective leaders know that plans are best accomplished with maximum participation. Thus, Moses involved the people in building the tabernacle.

First, he gathered them together and shared the overall vision and plan with them. "Then Moses assembled all the congregation of the sons of Israel, and said to them, 'These are the things that the LORD has commanded you to do'" (Ex. 35:1).

Second, he told them how they could participate in the plans. Some could participate financially: "Take from among you a contribution to the LORD" (Ex. 35:5). Others participated by working: "Let every skilled man among you come, and make all that the LORD has commanded" (Ex. 35:10). Some worked at the actual building, others gave financially, and many prayed for its successful completion. But all had ownership in the vision.

The Principle of Resource Utilization

In order for the people of Israel to build the tabernacle, they needed numerous resources: treasure, talent, time, and spirit.

Treasure

How did Moses get the financial assistance needed? He asked!

First, he instructed the people to ask the Egyptians for assistance. "Now the sons of Israel had done according to the word of Moses, for they had requested from the Egyptians articles of silver and articles of gold, and clothing" (Ex. 12:35). God granted the Israelites favor so the Egyptians gave them what was needed for the tabernacle.

Then Moses asked the people themselves to give. At first the people might have thought the gifts from the Egyptians were for their own keeping. However, they eventually realized that God wanted to use a large portion of those gifts to build the tabernacle. Following Moses' request, "everyone whose heart stirred him and everyone whose spirit moved him came and brought the LORD's contribution for the work of the tent of meeting" (Ex. 35:21). In fact the response of the people was so overwhelming that Moses had to tell them to stop bringing gifts. "Thus the people were restrained from bringing any more" (Ex. 36:6). Sometimes the financial resources are at hand, and you only need to ask.

> A church grows when it effectively utilizes its resources of prayer, people, time, and money.

Talent

There is more to obtaining results than just creating a plan; someone has to do the work. Though we often think of spiritual gifts as a New Testament phenomenon, the Spirit also gifted people in the Old Testament. God told Moses that he had gifted several people as craftsmen for building the tabernacle. Speaking of Bezalel, God said,

I have filled him with the Spirit of God in wisdom, in understanding, in knowledge, and in all kinds of craftsmanship, to make artistic designs for work in gold, in silver, and in bronze, and in the cutting of stones for settings, and in the carving of wood, that he may work in all kinds of craftsmanship. (Ex. 31:3–5)

Once the financial resources were gathered, Moses called "every skillful person in whom the LORD had put skill, everyone whose heart stirred him, to come to the work to perform it" (Ex. 36:2).

Time

Treasure and talent are necessary resources, but we must not forget another important resource: time. While we do not know the exact amount of time it took to build the tabernacle—from the reception of the plan to gathering of resources to construction to completion—we do know it occurred within a forty year period of time. The amount of time required depends on how large a plan is conceived, but several principles regarding time should be kept in mind.

First, the more long-range the plan, the more tentative the plan is. Long-range plans require flexibility. Plans that will not be finished for three or more years should be held lightly; that is, they need few details. They are so far in the future that any details put down today may need to be changed as time goes by.

Second, the more short-range the plan, the more specific the plan needs to be. Short-range plans require firmness. Plans that will be finished in less than two years should be held tightly; that is, they need specific details. Planning needs to increase in specificity as the event draws closer. The less time available for goal realization, the greater the specificity required in the plan.

Third, plans may be put into action before all the details are complete. Plans should not be looked on as works of art or objects of beauty. The key feature of a good plan is that it works—it gets the needed results. As people on the planning team gain enthusiasm, they will be eager to implement some aspects of the overall plan. Encourage them to do so. More will be accomplished in less time.

Fourth, time delay should be built into all plans. Do not build the plan so there is no flextime. Plans rarely work on their original time schedule. So, build in space to allow for unexpected delays.

Fifth, if it takes more time to plan than it will to implement the plan, it is taking too long. A few years ago, a friend of mine checked up on a church where he had helped them develop a five-year plan. To his amazement, the planning team was active seven years after the fact, still revising their original plan. They told him they hadn't gotten around to putting the plan into action yet, but they were still enjoying the planning process. That is too long! If it takes longer to design the plan than to actually do it, it is time to stop.

Spirit

Money we understand, personnel we understand, and time we understand, but too often we forget the necessary spiritual resources to fulfill a plan.

Plans create change and change always creates conflict. The situation was no different for Moses. While he was on the mountain receiving directions to build the tabernacle, resistance was forming in the camp. Since it took so long for Moses to come back with God's plan, the people started using their resources to build a golden calf, which was a spiritual turning away from God. "Now when the people saw that Moses delayed to come down from the mountain, the people assembled about Aaron and said to him, 'Come, make us a god who will go before us'" (Ex. 32:1). Observing the people from heaven, God told Moses that the people had "turned aside from the way which [God] commanded them" (32:8). This was a spiritual problem of huge proportions. Before the work could move forward, sin had to be confronted, confession made, and forgiveness granted. In other words, the people had to be in a proper relationship with God spiritually.

Undoubtedly, this is a difficult concept to get our minds around in a practical way. But, it is clear that seeing a plan through to completion takes more than tangible resources. It takes spiritual resources as well.

The Principle of Examination

If planning is to be effective, the effort applied should be commensurate with the results desired.

Plans do not accomplish themselves. It takes action on the part of leaders and workers to make things happen. Even though God provided Moses and his workers with detailed plans, someone still had to carve the silver, mold the gold, and sew the curtains. When the tabernacle was all finished, someone had to set it up. It was one thing to make it, quite another to put it all together.

After it was set up, it later had to be disassembled, carted around the desert, and reassembled each time the nation of Israel moved. Try to picture the people of Israel—about a million people—walking around the wilderness following a cloud. When the cloud stopped, it was time to set up the tabernacle. How was this organized? We do not know for sure. Yet our own experience leads us to believe that someone had to oversee the set up, maintenance, and tear down. Plans always demand that someone be in charge and hold others accountable for doing their jobs.

As an experienced leader once said, "It's not what is expected that gets done but what is inspected." In the case of the tabernacle, Moses was the inspector general. "So the sons of Israel did all the work according to all that the LORD had commanded Moses. And Moses examined all the work" (Ex. 39:42–43). In truth, there is no perfect plan. Therefore leaders must examine the plan, examine the workers, evaluate what is working and what is not, make adjustments, and move forward.

What is your tabernacle? It may not be as costly or as grand a design as that given to Moses. Indeed, it may not come directly from God's hand, nor will your plan likely have the explicit detail that Moses' plan entailed. The principles, however, will be the same. Develop your vision, put a plan into place, gain ownership, look for resources, and get on with the work.

MY PLANNING NOTEBOOK

Principles of Planning:

- Leadership is the ability to see reality, envision a preferred future, and design a plan that takes people forward.

My Comments:

- Planning is an investment rather than an expenditure of time.

My Comments:

- My plans are good plans; your plans are bad plans.

My Comments:

- A church grows when it effectively utilizes its resources of prayer, people, time, and money.

My Comments:

- It is not what is expected that gets done but what is inspected.

NOTES

1. C. Peter Wagner, *Your Church Can Grow* (Glendale, Calif.: Regal, 1976), 57.

2. Ed Stetzer and Mike Dodson, *Comeback Churches* (Nashville, Tenn.: Broadman & Holman, 2007), 210.

3. Ibid., 211.

Heroes and lone rangers are dead ducks.
The real power is in capturing and utilizing
the talent of diverse players to meet the
organization's fundamental goals.

—PETER DIGIAMMARINO

FIVE

Team Together

anish philosopher Søren Kierkegaard told the story of a man who wanted to jump a ditch. To get a long run at it, he backed up, and then backed up some more. He took such a long run that, when he finally got to the ditch, he was too tired to jump over it.

I have heard similar stories from church leaders concerning their attempts to plan for the future. They use so much energy planning that they never put the plan into action. The problem is that leaders often try to do all the planning themselves. Instead, they should use the planning process as an opportunity to involve other people so that the entire congregation owns the plan. A friend of mine likes to say TEAM stands for Together Everyone Accomplishes More. He's right! If you hope to develop a plan that makes an impact on your church, you must involve others in the process.

Together
Everyone
Accomplishes
More

Team Building in the Bible

Team ministry is biblical. Many leaders in the Bible used a team ministry approach. Even leaders we might think operated alone actually had a team around them. For example, Moses operated with a team, which at various times included Aaron, Hur, Joshua, the twelve spies, and the seventy elders. Aaron assisted Moses in communicating to the people (Ex. 4:14 and following). Hur and Aaron supported Moses when physical exertion made him tired and weak (Ex. 17:8–13). Jethro counseled Moses when the work of ministry nearly swallowed him up (Ex. 18:13–23). Leading a million people was no easy task. Moses needed a team to accomplish what God had called him to do.

King David also surrounded himself with a team of godly people (2 Sam. 23:8–39). During his exile, several team members continued to support David: men like Ittai, Zadok, Abiathar, Hushai, Ziba, and Abishai (2 Sam. 15:19—16:4). David even submitted himself to a fellow team member who confronted him about sin (2 Sam. 12:1–7).

To rebuild the wall of Jerusalem, Nehemiah knew he must assemble a capable team to labor together. A few of his team members included Ezra (Neh. 8:1–9), Hanani, Hanaiah (Neh. 7:1–2), Shelemiah, Zadok, Pedaiah, and Hanan (Neh. 13:13).

The New Testament also provides illustrations of team ministry. Perhaps the most well-known team in the Bible is Jesus and his disciples (Matt. 10:1; Mark 3:14; 6:31–34; Luke 6:12–16; 9:1). Paul was a prominent leader, but he too ministered with a team. His coworkers included Barnabas, John Mark, Timothy, Titus, Erastus, and Silas (Acts 19:22; Rom. 16:1–15, 21–23; Col. 4:7–14; 2 Tim. 4:10–13).

Team ministry flows from the precepts and practices of God's leaders in both the Old and New Testaments. Teams form the foundation for effective ministry in every age but especially during times of change. Moses used a team as the people relocated from Egypt to the Promised Land. Jesus used a team to found the Church. Paul used a team to take the gospel to the ends of the Gentile world. It is not surprising that Solomon wisely claims that wisdom comes with "many advisors" (Prov. 11:14; 15:22; 24:6 NIV) and that "two are better than one" (Eccl. 4:9–12 NIV).

Implementing a Planning Team

Teamwork is crucial to developing a plan for the future of your church. Church leaders who desire to increase their ministry fruitfulness by using a planning team often ask one or more of the following questions.

Who Does the Planning?

The size of the church often determines who does the planning. In smaller churches the dominant control over planning is generally found in the key families and groups of people who have served in the church the longest. People who have kept the church alive through their hard work and wealth are the *de facto* planners. Nothing significant is done in the church without their full support.

In medium-sized churches, planning is most often carried out by a group of committees, with the finance committee being the most influential. Depending on church polity, this might be a board of trustees, deacons, or other named council.

Planning in larger churches is usually in the hands of the senior pastor and staff. A single church board will also have a final say in any comprehensive plan, but for the most part the actual designing of the plan is left to the paid staff.

Whether planning is controlled by families, committees, or paid staff has a major impact on how planning is accomplished. Lyle E. Schaller notes five generalizations as to how planning is shaped by those in control of the planning process:

(1) When the greatest control over the allocation of resources is vested in the finance committee or the trustees, this often is associated with congregations that are declining in size. (2) When the control is largely in the hands of persons who have been members of the church for 15 years or longer, this often is related to a strong desire to recreate yesterday. (3) When the greatest control is vested in program committees, such as worship, education, music, evangelism, and social action, this is likely to result in the greatest degree of creativity. (4) When the largest single quantity of control is lodged in the nominating committee, this frequently means that maintenance of the institution will be placed at the top of the priority list. (5) When the pastor is the most influential driving force in the congregation, it is not long before the priorities begin to reflect his or her special gifts and major concerns.[1]

In larger churches, the planning process is usually the domain of the senior pastor, the paid staff, and the main church board. While day-to-day, week-to-week, or month-to-month planning is often done at lower administrative levels, the upper levels of church staff typically design long-range plans. This executive model of planning is more effective in larger churches than in smaller ones that are tightly controlled by influential laypersons. Whether the pastor is the primary voice or one voice among many, it is important to involve others in the planning process for at least two reasons.

First, churches are volunteer organizations. Members attend, participate, and withdraw any time they desire to do so. No matter what your church's polity, worship attendees vote every week with their attendance, tithes and offerings, and willingness to volunteer in service. For this reason, the congregation always maintains a huge measure of control. To obtain full support of the congregation for a master plan, the congregation needs to be engaged and provided the opportunity to offer input in the design of the plan.

Second, volunteer organizations function best when members are united around a central guiding priority supported by measurable and attainable goals. When goals are thrust on volunteers without first giving them the opportunity to offer input or feedback, volunteers often find it difficult to embrace the goals or work hard to achieve them. The old adage is true: "My goals are good goals; your goals are bad goals." Hence, those expected to support the goals must have a say in their development. For these and other reasons, many churches find it best to pull together a planning team to guide the master planning process. However, the planning team should have a good mix of church leaders and volunteers.

Should an Existing Board or Committee Be Used?

Using existing boards and committees as the planning team is usually not a good idea. Such governing groups are used to fixing problems and find it difficult to develop creative new ideas that build a church for the future. Most church committees are good at discussing ideas, maintaining the church institution, delegating authority, and handling conflict. They are not as good at innovation and creative planning. Generally speaking, church boards and committees focus on the problems of the church, seeking to maintain the institution through management of conflict and limited resources. Church committees and boards are rarely able to identify a new rallying cry or vision for the future of a church. Thus, when you pull together a special planning team, you create a fresh opportunity to innovate new ideas for future growth.

Who Should Be on the Planning Team?

It is good to have people on the planning team who can help get the plan accomplished after it is finished. However, to get new ideas, it is crucial to involve some new people. The general rule is if you want things to stay the same, recruit long-term members or attendees to be on the team. However, if you want things to change, involve new people. New people on the team help the group avoid *groupthink*. Groupthink is the tendency of groups who have been together a long time to think the same. If you honestly want to continuously improve your current ministry and dream new dreams for the future, you must allow for new thinking, which means involving new people in the planning process.

Who Should Chair the Planning Team?

Avoid the tendency to think that only church board members should chair the planning team. This is an antiquated idea developed in an era when few people were well-educated or had leadership experience. Using only elected board or committee members as a chair person sometimes places people in roles for which they have no gifting, burns out overworked board members, and excludes a large number of potential church members from serving.

It is best not to have the chairperson elected by church vote, nor to have the assembled planning team select its own chair. Using either of these methods almost assures the selection of an ingrown committee person who has a take charge personality, little skill at team building, little creativity, and more commitment to the process than actual effectiveness.

> In most churches, the pastor should appoint the
> chairperson of the planning team.

From my experience, it is best to find a person who has the ministry giftedness, the passions, and the leadership skills for leading a planning team. In general, you should look for someone who is able to lead adults, has no axe to grind about past issues, cares about the ministry direction of the church, and is able to build unity. In most situations, the lead pastor should appoint the chairperson after consultation with the main church board members.

How Should the Team Be Organized?

Several decades ago, researchers discovered that a person's approach to problem solving could be located on a continuum between the extremes of high adaption and high innovation.[2] People who are highly adaptive strive to make existing organizations better. Such people often work in fields like medicine, accounting, and various types of clerical jobs. Each of these jobs requires people who can fix what is wrong with an existing system. Adaptors are naturally best at implementation. While adaptors bring stability to an organization, they are not always good at thinking creatively.

On the opposite pole of the continuum are innovators. Those who are highly innovative prefer to work in fields where creativity is expected. In contrast to adaptors, innovators seek to make existing systems different. They like to serve in areas where they can develop new products and bring fresh insights to bear on old problems. Innovators often work in research and development, sales and marketing, or financial arenas (not accounting). Innovators are naturally gifted at generating ideas. Since innovators are agents of change, they are easily frustrated when planning takes longer than it should.

Neither of these types of individuals ought to be viewed as right or wrong. In fact most people fall into one of these two categories by the age of two and remain consistent over time. As far as research has determined, there is no cultural, gender, or birth order bias. People just tend to prefer being adaptive or creative.

Applying this research to church ministry, some people are passionate about improving the current church ministry. This is often called *continuous improvement*. If you ask these people to dream about the future of the church, they just cannot seem to do it. They see the present picture very well, but have a hard time thinking long-term for the future. So instead of trying to force them to envision the future of a church's ministry, it is best to let them focus on what they find easy to do—improving the present. On the other hand, some people like to dream about what a church can become in the next few years. They really enjoy projecting ideas into the future. If they are asked to work on improving the present, they are bored. So it is best to let them focus on how to build the future of the church.

Thus, you should consider dividing your team into two subunits: a present team and a future team. Using two teams—one looking at the present and the other at the future—is a simple idea, but few churches do it. Part of the reason is that the pressures of the present situation are so demanding it causes churches to invest great energy into preserving what they are already doing, rather than designing the future. The old proverb is true: "It's hard to make plans to drain the swamp when the alligators are biting."

The idea for using two teams comes from Ken Blanchard, a popular business consultant. He suggests dividing into two teams that he calls a P Team and an F Team. As you might suspect, *P* stands for present, and *F* stands for future. The P Team builds on a church's core values to see if current ministries may be improved. The F Team looks to create the future.

So how do you decide who works better on which team? The best way is to enter into a brief conversation with leaders and ask them to answer the following questions:

- Would you rather dream about the future or fix the present?
- Would you rather design a new program or improve an existing one?
- Would you rather do the right things or do things right?
- Would you rather be innovative or effective?
- Would you rather develop ministry for future members or develop ministry for members who are already here?

As you might guess, the first part of each question is slanted toward people who would fit best on the F Team. The second half of each question indicates people who would fit best on the P Team.

Try to enlist fifteen people on the long-range planning team—fourteen members and one chairperson. These fifteen are then divided into two sub-teams of seven people each—six members and one leader. It looks like this.

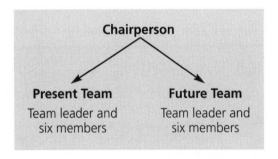

The total number of members on a planning team should be relatively small. The larger a church grows, the fewer the people involved on the actual planning team. The team will work hard to gain a wide base of input and support, but the team itself ought to be small. In the great majority of churches, a team of seven is more than enough to get the job done. A planning team becomes less effective in proportion to the increase in size over seven members. Thus, using two sub-teams of seven people is an effective way to work.

What Does a Sub-Team Actually Do?

The P Team asks two main questions: *Where are we?* and *How are we doing?* The F Team asks two different questions: *Where are we going?* and *How are we going to get there?* To clarify the difference between the two teams even more, look at the following chart.

P Team Asks	F Team Asks
Where are we?	Where are we going?
How are we doing?	How are we going to get there?
What are the church's needs?	What are the community's needs?
What needs to be improved?	What needs to be developed?
What are the problems?	What are the opportunities?
How do we train current leaders?	How do we add new leadership?
What are the church's demographics?	What are the community's demographics?
How do we involve members?	How do we reach new people?
What are the internal issues?	What are the external issues?
What are the rules?	How can we break the rules?
How can we preserve the present?	How can we seize the future?
How can we manage the process?	How can we lead the parade?
What is probable?	What is possible?
How can we satisfy our members?	How can we amaze our members?
How can we fine-tune the ministry?	How can we create a new ministry?

How Do the Two Sub-Teams Work Together?

The two sub-teams come together in two ways. First, sometimes you can assign one of the teams to a particular project. For instance, you might assign the P Team to look at the visitor follow-up process. They would then take a detailed look at how visitors are currently being followed up, perhaps visit with other churches to see what they are doing in this area, and then suggest some ways to improve your current process. Of course, you could also assign the F Team to look at visitor follow-up. However, they would look at the future in an attempt to project how visitors' attitudes might change in the next five to ten years, and then project ideas on how to design a totally new approach to reaching newcomers. In both situations, the teams function as project teams focusing on only one segment of our church ministry.

Then, every two to three years, it is wise to do a complete long-range plan for the entire church. In this instance, the P Team takes an audit of the entire church program and makes extended recommendations for improving the entire church ministry. The F Team looks at the future and makes broad recommendations on what new ministries the church must start to be effective in the future. In this manner, the two sub-teams serve the large process of long-range planning.

How Is the Planning Team Selected?

Several approaches to selecting the planning team can be used. One approach in smaller churches is to select a wide representation of people from the congregation. While this will give voice to a wide range of viewpoints, it often ends up creating a team that is too large to accomplish its goal. In addition, it normally results in an over-representation of old-timers and maintenance personnel (trustees, financial officers, and building committee members) on the planning team. The result of such a team is few new ideas, dreams, or plans for the future. Instead the planning team will probably attempt to recreate yesterday. In the great number of cases, such a team will just bore the congregation with watered-down ideas.

A better idea is to appoint a smaller planning team with a large representation of new people. In contrast to a team chosen by representative vote, an appointed team will have a greater capacity for developing a creative new central thrust to excite and unite the congregation for future growth. In short, if you want things to remain the same, choose a large planning team made up of representatives from every sphere of the congregation. If you want change, appoint a small select group of future-oriented people who share the same value system.

At the very least, the planning team should have 20 percent newer members. If your church has a lot of newcomers, select people who have been in the church for less than two years. If your church has few newcomers, select those who have been in the church less than five years. If you do not have any newcomers who have come in the last five years, your church has other problems and would benefit greatly from the assistance of a church consultant.

What Is the Pastor's Role?

In larger congregations, it is generally expected that the lead pastor initiate the planning process. Members of large churches look to the pastor to set the overall direction for the congregation. Large church pastors are expected to cast vision. If they do not suggest new directions, the people sense something is awry.

The smaller a church is the less influence a pastor exerts on the planning process. Pastors of smaller churches generally cannot produce change, but they can introduce change. For example, the pastor of a small church can suggest the need for a master plan, but the key people will have to make it happen. By contrast, in a larger church, a pastor may be able to just appoint a long-range planning team in an *ad hoc* manner.

Whether in a large, a medium, or a small church, it is the pastor's role to assist the church to plan for the future. The level of involvement by the pastor in the planning process will depend on the pastor's giftedness, personality, and skill set. Some pastors have the ability to lead a church in planning, but others do not. Some pastors are discouraged, while others are excited about the future. Some pastors are coasting to retirement, yet others are working hard. All these aspects will influence the specific involvement of a pastor on the planning team.

Schaller suggests that the pastors who are most helpful to a planning team have the following abilities:

To distinguish between planning and decision-making, to help the [team] see that its role as a planning body is to identify and evaluate alternatives rather than to act as a decision-making group; to identify and affirm assets, resources and strengths, and to encourage the [team] to build on these assets in planning for an expansion of ministry; to bring a contagious note of hope to the [team's] deliberations; to inspire the members to look toward tomorrow rather than to seek to do yesterday over again.[3]

Generally speaking, the longer tenure a pastor has in a particular church, the more influence he or she will have on the planning process. When a pastor is new to a congregation, the church leaders hold the power for planning, but as they gain trust and confidence in the pastor throughout a number of years, they tend to release some of the planning power. Other variables include, but are not limited to:

- the tradition or custom of the congregation (lay-run or staff-run),
- the age of the congregation (newer congregation or older congregation), and
- the actual focus of the planning (ends or means).

Pastors have the most influence on master planning in staff-run, newer congregations. For example, when a church is rethinking its mission or role or new outreach thrusts, the pastor will have a large say. Pastors have less influence in lay-run, older congregations where issues of means are concerned. For example, when a church is considering a relocation or construction of new buildings or finances, the pastor will have less of a say.

The locus of control over the planning process will have a major impact on mapping the future of your church. Who do you want to shape your church's direction for the coming five to ten years? The answer to that question points out who should be on the planning team. Be sure to choose wisely.

MY PLANNING NOTEBOOK

Selecting the planning team:

- TEAM stand for Together Everyone Accomplishes More.

- Team ministry is crucial for developing ownership of the plan, particularly during times of change.

- Rather than using existing boards or committees, we should pull together a new group of people to be on the planning team.

- If we want things to stay the same, we should select long-term members to be on the team. However, if we want things to change, we should involve newer people.

- The pastor should appoint a chairperson who has the skills to lead the planning team.

- Divide the team into two sub-teams: a present team and a future team.

- Ask the present team to focus on what needs to happen to make the current ministry better. Ask the future team to focus on what needs to happen to make the ministry effective in the future.

- The people on the planning team will have a major impact on the future of our church. Who do we want on this team? Who should not be on this team? We need to choose wisely.

My Comments:

NOTES

1. Lyle E. Schaller, "Planning or Decision-Making?," *The Christian Ministry* (Chicago: The Christian Century Foundation, September 1981), 10.

2. M.J. Kirton, ed., "A Theory of Cognitive Style," *Adaptors and Innovators: Styles of Creativity and Problem Solving* (New York: Routledge, 1994).

3. Schaller, 12.

Study the past. Live the moment. Plan the future.
—AUTHOR UNKNOWN

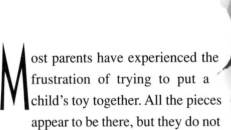

SIX

Look Around

Most parents have experienced the frustration of trying to put a child's toy together. All the pieces appear to be there, but they do not seem to go together as the instruction manual indicates.

In a similar way, church leaders sometimes find it frustrating when they try to put the pieces of ministry together so that the church experiences renewed growth and vitality. While there are only three major pieces of church ministry that must be put together, each piece has several sub-pieces, which makes the process more complex.

Discern Your Church

The first phase in putting the pieces together is to discern the church's ministry. Church leaders should follow four steps in this phase.

First, look at the church's *history*. Look all the way back to the founding of the church and note the major events—good and bad. Seek to understand the church's unique DNA, such as the specific core values that have characterized the ministry over its entire lifetime.

Second, chart the last ten years of *worship attendance*. Observe the basic trends of growth, decline, or plateauing. Graphing your church's worship attendance gives an excellent indication of its health. For example, notice how the attendance graphs of the two churches below point out the relative health of each one. While the graphs do not tell the entire story, they do raise a number of questions that a planning team should discuss.

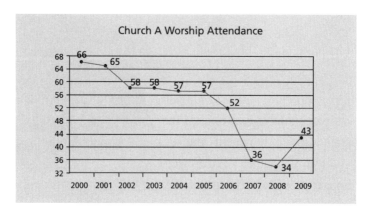

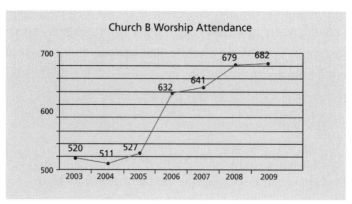

Third, analyze the church's *growth history*, especially the last ten years. Determine the church's general direction of growth. Using the average annual growth rate over the last ten years, project the trajectory of your church's growth or decline into the future if things do not change. Notice the projections of Church A and Church B below.

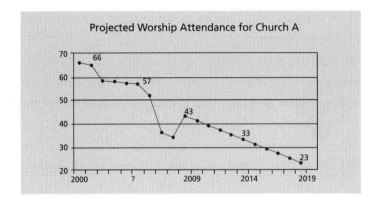

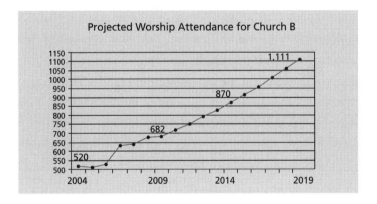

This analysis points out the danger Church A is facing. If something is not done to change its basic direction, it appears to be headed for continued decline and eventual closure. In contrast, Church B is heading upward. A planning team will want to make changes to accommodate the potential growth of this church.

Fourth, make a list of all the things that are *working* and that are *not working* in the church's ministry. What are your church's strengths and weaknesses? What must be done to improve the current ministry? What must be done to prepare for the next ten years?

Discern Your Community

The second phase in putting the pieces together focuses on the community around the church.

First, study the general *demographic trends* to discover what is happening around your church. Ask some of the following questions: What is the average age of people in your community? What is the educational level of those in your community? Who is moving in and out? How well does your church's demographic makeup match that of your community? What does this say about the future ministry of your church?

Second, survey the *needs* and *concerns* in your community. What are the major challenges being faced by people? What are the interests of people in your general area? What are people concerned about?

Third, interview *community leaders*. Talk with members of the local media to find out their perspectives on your community. Speak with business and government leaders, as well as realtors, developers, and other members of your community. What do these leaders say about the challenges and possibilities for your community?

Fourth, identify potential *ministry opportunities*. Based on what you discover about your community, identify at least three areas where your church could serve the community in a missional manner. What resources has God provided to your church that can be used to meet the challenges faced in your community?

Fifth, identify possible *growth barriers*. What social, ethnic, cultural, economic, educational, psychological, emotional, or geographic barriers will your church face in the next ten years? Begin to plan on how your church will respond to these barriers.

Use a SWOT Analysis

One of the most helpful tools for discerning a church and its community is the application of a SWOT analysis. The four letters stand for the following categories:

Strengths: aspects of a church that help achieve its mission.

Weaknesses: aspects of a church that hinder achieving its mission.

Opportunities: external possibilities around the church that could be helpful in achieving its mission.

Threats: external conditions around the church that might be harmful in achieving its mission.

The planning team can employ a SWOT analysis by asking the following four questions:

1. What are the strengths of our church?
2. What are the weaknesses of our church?
3. What opportunities for ministry exist for our church?
4. What threats or obstacles hinder our church from taking advantage of these opportunities?

The answers to these four questions can then be plotted on a chart similar to the one below to give a visual overview of the church.

	Helpful	Harmful
Internal	Strengths	Weaknesses
External	Opportunities	Threats

Discern Your Direction

The third phase in putting the pieces together builds on the first two phases above.

First, *pray* for insight and wisdom from the Holy Spirit. Call church leaders and other participants to times of prayer, asking God to direct your thinking for the future. Remember it is God's direction you are seeking; make prayer a major part of discerning your church's future.

Second, look to the *Bible* for insight into what God's desires are for your church. God's will is communicated through his written Word. Take time to study what he has already said regarding the character of a congregation and its purpose.

Third, consider your church's historic *DNA*. It is nearly impossible for a church to change its DNA. Therefore, it is most fruitful to develop your future based on how God has created your church. Work with your church's uniqueness, rather than against it.

Fourth, taking everything into consideration, write a *vision* for the future of your church. What do you sense is God's hope, dream, and vision for your church? What new ministries do you need to create in the next few years to reach your community for Christ? What changes must you make in the current ministry to remain alive and vibrant?

Fifth, design a *plan* that will lead your church to fulfill God's vision for it. Decide what must happen first, second, and so forth. Set target dates for accomplishing your goals. Get started, and then monitor your progress.

As you begin to fit these three ministry pieces—church, community, and direction—into place, that pile of loose ministry parts will begin to look more like an achievable plan for the future.

MY PLANNING NOTEBOOK

Evaluating Our Church:

- Discern our church's ministry by looking at our past history and graphing our worship attendance for the last ten years.

My Comments:

- Discern our community by studying the local demographics and surveying community leaders.

My Comments:

- Conduct a SWOT analysis to identify future opportunities and threats to our ministry.

My Comments:

- Discern our direction, taking into prayerful consideration what we discover about our church and community.

Growing churches tend to believe that the most desirable forms of ministry are outreach, not in reach.

—GEORGE BARNA

SEVEN

Reach Out

In the early growth years of the automobile industry, Henry Ford got a leg up on the competition by using standardized parts and mass production techniques. He found that by building only one type of car, he could produce them quickly and inexpensively. Ford's Model T was affordable, met most people's needs, and made his company the premier automobile manufacturer of the time.

It did not stay that way for long. Gradually, people started desiring different models and colors of cars. Unfortunately, Henry Ford was not interested in reaching out to meet people where they were. His response to people's requests for different colors was, "People can buy any color car they want, as long as it's black." By refusing to put people first, Ford caused his company to fall from its number one position in car manufacturing as it lost market share to other auto manufacturers. If only he had been willing to put people first.

As your church crafts a new plan for the future, you must put people first. This is only common sense. Church ministry is a social process, a web of interactions between people. Putting people first tends to reinforce the desire and commitment of people to serve each other. This phenomenon is called the *virtuous circle*, meaning that when people are put first, they tend to feel more satisfied with their church. They communicate this to others and tend to put other people first in their own contacts, thus keeping the circle of service flowing from one person to another.

A Most Important Question

The Peter F. Drucker Foundation suggests that a major question all non-profit organizations (including churches) need to ask is, "Who is our customer?"

Granted most of us are not accustomed to thinking of people who attend or visit our church as customers. The definition of the term *customer* usually refers to someone who buys something from us on a regular basis. This usage does not fit the church well since we are not selling anything. Our church is in the service business. We serve others by giving them the free gospel of Jesus Christ.

However, the secondary meaning of *customer* refers to those with whom we have regular contact. This is an appropriate usage for the church since we do have regular dealings with people. Actually every company or organization has its own unique term for customer. Doctors call them patients, attorneys call them clients, and churches call them members and guests. Perhaps the word *constituency* fits the church better than *customer*. But no matter which word we choose to use, serving people is what churches are called to do.

To do the best job of putting people first, we must identify and understand the people we serve. A startling example of this is found in Acts 6. The church in Jerusalem was growing quickly, and the people had an organized means of serving one another. Most were extremely happy but, as it turned out, one group was being overlooked. The Hellenistic Jews felt that their widows were not being served well by the church.

The disciples and other church leaders had made the mistake of thinking they were serving only one group of customers, when in actuality two very different groups needed to be served. By identifying a different segment of people, the disciples were able to develop a plan to serve all their constituents well. They were able to put people first in their church, because they had identified their unique needs and expectations and adjusted their ministry to serve them.

Every church needs to serve at least two main customers: people inside the church and people outside the church. Technically our internal customers represent those who already call our church home, whether they are members or regular worshipers. Our internal customers are easily identified and served. We most likely already have their names and addresses in our church records. The weekly contact we have with each other gives us inside clues on how to serve one another.

Our external customers are people who could attend our church if the appropriate circumstance existed. These external customers represent a group that is at least six times larger than our internal customer group. They are the friends, family members, and acquaintances of our worshipers. They are the people who drive by our church daily on their way to work. They are the people we are trying to reach with the good news of Jesus Christ.

Who Goes First?

Since we have two groups of customers—internal and external— where do we place the priority in our planning efforts? It is not always an easy answer. Christ called to us to care for each other inside the church as well as reach the lost. It is not an either/or situation but a both/and one. That is why your team is divided into an F Team and a P Team. The P Team zeros in on your internal customers (members and regular attendees), while the F Team centers on your external customers (people outside your church).

In some cases, it is necessary to begin by focusing on people inside your church. I found this out while pastoring a church in Portland, Oregon. I had arrived at the church with the intention of focusing on outreach and evangelism. After getting acquainted with the people, I soon learned that little fellowship or support had taken place among the members for several years.

One evening as the deacons and I were preparing to visit some church members, I specifically asked the chairman of the deacon board to ride with me to the homes of some members. My desire was twofold. I wanted to get to know this gentleman better; I also figured he would know most of the people and could direct me to their homes and introduce me to those I had not already met. I handed him three cards with the names and addresses of members I wanted to visit. He glanced through the cards, looked at me and commented, "Pastor, I don't know where any of these people live."

Surprised, I replied that I thought after so many years at the church he would know everyone (the church was not very big).

Embarrassed he mumbled back, "Pastor, I've been in this church fifteen years and I've never been in the home of any other church members but those of my own family."

From that experience, I knew I needed to change my strategy. Before I could lead this church in reaching out to its external customers, I needed to help them begin getting to know each other. How could they reach those outside the church when they could not even talk to each other in their own homes?

If our internal customers feel good about our church and know how to care for each other, then they will do a much better job of serving our external customers. Many churches planning to develop an outreach ministry will need to focus first on building care among those already in the church.

Other churches will find that their congregations already know how to love and care for each other. Their people are putting each other first in very practical ways. In such a case, it will be fine to place the emphasis on those outside the church. But unless this is the case, it will do no good to reach out to people and attempt to bring them into a church that does not already demonstrate the values you hope to convey. Newcomers will see through such hypocrisy quickly.

Put People First

Reaching out means treating people the way they expect to be treated. It is best to treat people with courtesy and respect. If we hope to build a church that offers excellent service, we need to be polite. Putting people first is not just a program; it is an attitude, a way of life. Putting people first means we listen to them. This means taking the time to informally talk with people as well as being reasonably available to them for appointments. It means taking their concerns seriously and responding appropriately.

We put people first when we provide ministry on their time schedules. If people are working Sunday, we may provide a service for them on a weeknight. Now, do we do everything a person wants? Probably not. It must fit our mission, vision, values, and goals. We must have the ability to do it in terms of resources. We may have to honestly admit that we would like to accommodate someone, but at this time, we simply cannot do it. But, our intent throughout is to serve by putting people first as much as we possibly can.

We put people first when we provide them with a phone number to call in case of emergencies. In a smaller church, all members should have the home phone numbers of the pastoral staff and church leaders. When a church gets larger, a senior pastor should give his or her home phone number to executive staff and main board members. Associate staff should give their phone numbers to people directly under their oversight or on committees that serve their ministry function. Small group leaders must give their phone numbers to the people in their small groups. Putting people first means we give people a way to get in touch with someone when they have a need. It does not have to be the senior pastor, but people in your church should have the home phone number of someone they may call if they have a need. You should want people to call you, no matter what time it is. They are your customers, and you need to serve them. When people call, it gives you a chance to maintain your relationship with them, and people really like to be served in this manner. Do not worry about people taking advantage of you. As a rule, they will only call if they honestly need help.

We put people first when we appreciate them. Most churches send a letter to visitors thanking them for attending, but how often do we thank our regular attendees for being faithful? Both are important ways to put people first. Whenever you learn that someone has gone out of their way to serve another person in your church, make certain it gets written up and made known. If you have a church newsletter, you can put a story in it. If not try this: Write up the act of service, have it framed, and give it to the other person publicly, reading the story to all present. Giving an award in this manner highlights the act of service and holds up your values for everyone to see.

We put people first when we serve their needs. Recognize that you cannot meet every need or every expectation, so you must prioritize the needs and expectations you will attempt to meet. To assure that you meet the expectations and needs of your customers, identify the three things that are most important to each group. Once you know what is important, you can then provide it. In practice, evangelism is targeted to external customers and focuses on their needs.

Churches which perceive unbelievers as their primary customer can use a chart showing concentric circles to communicate their idea of serving people outside the church best. New people are placed in the bull's-eye (the most valuable position), those closest to them in the next ring, on out to the last ring which is the paid staff. This is not a true organizational chart showing reporting relationships or functional divisions and organizational structure. Instead, the concentric chart tells everyone that the purpose of the church is to reach the unchurched. All decisions are to be made based on the reaching the unchurched person. It puts people first, in this case the unchurched person.

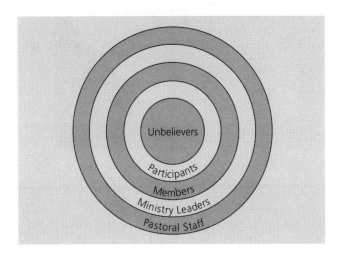

No church will put people first unless the pastoral staff and main leaders visibly and constantly commit themselves to the idea. Putting people first only happens if the people at the top lead the charge. When they do not set the example, everyone succumbs to the pressure of just doing church instead of serving one another.

Another way to understand the role of the planning team is that the P Team focuses on your internal customers, while the F Team focuses on the external customer. Neither team is more important than the other. They are both important. An underlying premise is that we can focus on our internal and external customers at the same time.

Seeing Opportunities

Taking hold of future opportunities and improving present ministries are equally challenging. There are unrealized opportunities in both arenas. Look at the following chart.

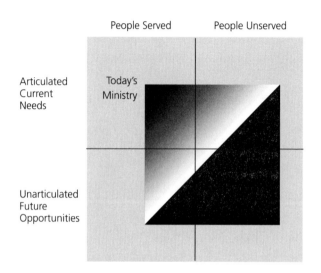

As you can see, the current ministry of most churches only serves those people whose needs have been articulated. There are still people left underserved, even though we know their needs. In addition, there is a vast area of unarticulated future opportunities that are not being served at all.

> Congregations that developed a plan to recruit members
> in the last year were much more likely to grow
> than congregations that had not.
> —C. KIRK HADAWAY

The following is a way to discover fresh opportunities to serve people.

First, make a list of people inside and outside of your church who are underserved in the chart above. Second, find a way to interview a representative sample of these people to discover some of their needs.

Third, make a list of at least three needs each group of people has that would be appropriate for your church to meet. Use a chart similar to the following to make your list.

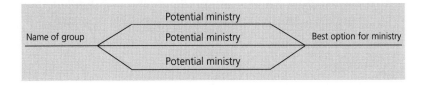

Through a process of discerning the community, one church discovered that the parents of young children were one of the underserved populations in their community. After interviewing a number of these families who did not attend church, three major needs surfaced: day care, marriage counseling, and ideas on how to keep the children off drugs. The church listed the three options on the chart as follows:

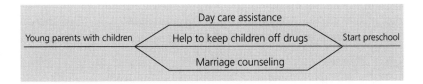

Through the process of discerning the church, the team determined that resources were not available to do marriage counseling or offer classes on keeping children off drugs. However, the church did have the resources—knowledge, money, personnel—to begin a preschool to offer day care assistance to young families in the community. The planning team determined that starting a preschool was the best, new option for serving this segment of the community around the church.

As your church conducts an analysis of both internal and external customers, it will detect new opportunities for ministry. Adding these new ministries to the planning process provides fresh energy for future growth. Remember: It takes new ministries to reach new people.

MY PLANNING NOTEBOOK

Reaching New People:

- Our church must serve internal customers (our current worshipers) and external customers (those outside our church).

My Comments:

- Growing churches place a priority on potential customers, i.e.: evangelism of those outside the church.

My Comments:

- It takes new ministries to reach new people.

Learning and innovation go hand in hand. The arrogance of success is to think that what you did yesterday will be sufficient for tomorrow.

—WILLIAM POLLARD

EIGHT

Keep It Fresh

Most New Year's resolutions are driven by a desire to rein in bad habits—to not eat as much junk food, to not spend so much money, to not watch as much TV. We commit to losing weight, living on a budget, or spending more time with loved ones.

A friend of mine, who is in her fifties and has done a lot in her life, made a unique kind of resolution this year. She resolved to do more new things. Yes, to do more things for the first time. Realizing she needed to be purposeful about introducing new things into her life, rather than only moderating what she was already doing, my friend made a commitment to try something each month she had never done.

I loved my friend's idea and admired her desire to stretch herself with new experiences. She aptly recognized the ease with which we keep doing the same things—and the intentionality required to keep things fresh.

Similar dynamics are at play in many churches. We are committed to being godly people and recognize the discipline it takes to maintain a healthy relationship with God, but we grow accustomed to doing ministry the same way month after month, year after year. If we experience any degree of success with a ministry, we are even more inclined to keep things the same in the future. But in doing things the same way over many years, we forget what it feels like to do or try new things. In essence, we create comfortable and safe ruts that prevent us from experiencing new and exciting places in ministry.

Why Change Is Needed

That is not to say we should change ministry plans and strategies just for the sake of change. People have enough to worry about and do not need the burden of constantly changing ministries in the church to keep up with the church across town or to adopt the latest ministry trend. There are two primary reasons, though, why it is necessary to keep things fresh and make changes in a church ministry.

To Improve Existing Ministries

Sometimes change is a means to improve current ministries. Perhaps there are problems with the way things are being done or there are obstacles that need to be overcome for the ministry to be effective or to grow. People usually sense the need for change in such situations, even if they cannot articulate what they are feeling. They may not be able to identify the problem area or have insight into how to address the problem. In fact, they may not be particularly open to making changes and may initially respond to ideas and proposals for improving the ministry with criticism or negativity. But most people will eventually embrace changes that lead to further effectiveness and growth.

For example, a Thursday evening Bible study for working women was experiencing low attendance. Thursday turned out to be a difficult night for many of the women, because they were already exhausted from the work week. Those who did manage to attend often fell asleep during the teaching! When the leaders of the group surveyed the women about which night of the week they preferred to meet, they learned that Tuesday night would work much better than Thursday, because it was earlier in the week when women felt more rested.

Even though the decision to move the Bible study to Tuesday night was based on the direct feedback received in the survey and resulted in improved attendance, it was still not a popular decision. Several women voiced concern and disapproval about the change. Ultimately, though, the change was necessary to improve the Bible study experience (increase attendance and enjoyment), and the group experienced growth and new life because of that change.

To Respond to Changing Situations

Change is necessary not only to improve ministries, but also to create new ministries in response to changing dynamics. This need for change may not be as obvious, because people in a church often are slow to see that the needs their ministry once met no longer exist in the same way. Sometimes the demographic in the surrounding community changes so that the community has different spiritual needs than it once had. Other times the demographic inside the church shifts, causing ministries that once thrived to become stuck in maintenance mode. Sometimes new systems or ministries in other areas of the church unintentionally render an existing ministry irrelevant or obsolete. Whatever the circumstances that are driving the change, effective leaders respond to evolving circumstances, often by creating new ministries to meet the new needs.

For example, a church had an extensive tape ministry for many years and at one point had paid staff and volunteers dedicated to this ministry. As time went on, however, the demand for tapes decreased, while the demand for CDs increased. Eventually, as technology progressed, the church started posting sermons online, making them available for download. Most people no longer saw the need to purchase a hard copy, so the once-thriving tape ministry became a thing of the past.

To evaluate the demise of the tape ministry, the church could ask several questions:

- Was there something wrong with the tape ministry? *No.*
- Were there inherent problems in the way the tape ministry was run? *Not necessarily.*
- Was there a societal shift in the way people preferred to listen to a message? *Certainly—advancements in technology shifted the preferences and needs of the average churchgoer.*

In order to accommodate the changing preferences of the congregation, it was necessary for the church to create a new kind of ministry.

Changes like this usually occur over time and are much harder to identify or predict than ministries that simply need to be improved in quality or efficiency. Early indicators might be that attendance will start to decline or the ministry will stop attracting new people or younger people. Sometimes the congregation will be tempted to spiritualize the loss of attendance as a decline in interest or demand, even though the reasons for the shift in behavior reflect something other than a shift in the congregation's spiritual priorities. In the case of the tape ministry, one might hear comments like, "The young adults coming to church today are just not interested in hearing the sermon when they miss a Sunday." A closer look at the situation, however, reveals that young adults simply prefer to receive their teaching content in a much different format—reflecting a larger shift in culture that has very practical repercussions for the church.

> Innovation is the ability to see change as
> an opportunity rather than a threat.

How to Make Effective Ministry Changes

There are several reasons why change and ministry innovation are necessary. Most of us agree, on a theoretical level, that our churches would benefit from changes in our ministries. But how do we actually make changes that improve the ministry? How do we generate new ideas when we are busy overseeing the ministries we have or are so accustomed to a certain way of doing things?

The good news is that you do not need to hire all new pastoral staff to bring in fresh ideas or go into debt building a new ministry center to make innovative changes in your ministry. Most likely, you already have most of the resources you need to come up with new ideas to improve your ministries and respond to the changes your church is experiencing. Here are five simple and practical things you can do to foster creativity and innovation.

Create Dissonance through Exposure

You might think that creating dissonance is the last thing you want to do with your church—as if making changes is not controversial enough, now you are supposed to create discord or disunity among your leaders! Dissonance in many contexts is a negative thing, but when it comes to making changes in your church, dissonance can be your friend.

People get very used to the way things are done in their church. By exposing them to other ministries and alternative ways of doing things, you help them catch a vision for what your ministry could look like. Your leaders can see the potential of your church while developing a more realistic or objective picture of what is currently being done. This difference between what they see elsewhere and what they currently experience at church is called *dissonance*. Dissonance expands people's conceptual understanding of the possible, creates dissatisfaction with how things are, and serves as motivation to make changes.

Visiting churches in your area is a convenient way to expose your team to new ways of doing things, and it often has the added benefit of developing unity among the church community in your area. I recommend visiting churches slightly larger than your church. This means your team will observe a church that has already navigated some of the growth dynamics that are unique to a church your size. Plus, the church is probably functioning with a similar amount of resources as your church does. If you were to visit a mega-church or another church that is substantially larger than your church, you will gather some great ideas, but you will probably find those ideas difficult to implement in a church with far fewer resources. Instead of being encouraged and inspired, your leaders may end up discouraged when they try to implement the same quality of ministry with significantly fewer resources.

One way to make the most of a visit to another church is to meet with your leaders before going to the church to make a list of all the ministries you want to observe and the questions you hope to answer through your visit. After the visit, meet again as a team to share observations or ideas. Often, simply seeing another way of doing ministry will prompt additional ideas among your leaders. Be prepared to write down their feedback and record any new ideas that are mentioned. If the ministry you observed is very different from what you are currently doing or is hard to comprehend by observation alone, you might want to arrange with the staff of the other church to meet for a time of asking questions and hearing more detailed information on their ministry.

Sometimes this kind of observation can help your planning team to see more clearly the possibilities of what a ministry could do or be; at other times, it will simply help them pick up ideas on how to tweak or to adapt a current ministry. A church with a larger weekly attendance might have a greater capacity for using multi-media in their worship service than you do. Visiting this larger church could give your team an idea of what they might want to work toward in the future. However, if your church visits another church about the same size, they may notice that the service flows well and has seamless transitions between the elements of the service. This could help your team immediately incorporate new ideas and improve what is already being done.

If there are no thriving churches in your area, consider making a trip to a church that is part of the same denomination or association. Although denominational ties are not as strong today as they once were, churches of the same denomination often have a similar culture. This means the ideas you collect from churches of your denomination may be easier to implement. In addition, denominational leaders may be able to recommend a church that is thriving in the same ministry areas you are interested in learning about. If your church has no denominational affiliation, consider visiting similar independent or non-denominational churches that have a good reputation in your region of the country.

If visiting other churches is not an option, consider reading a ministry book together or attending a conference for church leaders. Meet at different points while reading the book or attending the conference to discuss, share insights, and hear from your team. This will expose your leaders to some new ways of thinking and help everyone discern what ideas could be applied in your context. If attending a conference, encourage your leaders to network and interact with people from other churches. This could help them to learn about new ideas, as well as establishing relational networks for encouragement and ideas in the future.

Investigate the Ministries of Larger Churches

Churches of any size can be innovative, but larger churches have the financial and pastoral resources to innovate and share new ideas for ministry. Their ideas are often extremely influential and have helped other churches develop more efficient and effective systems for evangelism, discipleship, membership, and service. For example, Willow Creek Community Church in South Barrington, Illinois, developed an evangelism training program called Contagious Christianity that has helped to train millions in the United States on how to share the gospel. Smaller churches could adopt this evangelism training program rather than attempting to create their own, freeing them to focus their time and energy on actually training adults in their church to share their faith. Saddleback Church in Lake Forest, California, developed a process for spiritual growth and maturity that many other churches adopted and now use to help their new members grow and get involved.

You and your team of leaders could investigate the ministries of mega-churches by visiting them on a Sunday or during the week, attending a conference presented by one of these churches, reading books published by their pastoral staff, or even doing some basic research online. It will not be difficult to access resources or information about most of these large churches, especially if they have been around for a few years and have a good reputation in the Christian community.

However, your challenge will be discerning what ideas will be relevant, applicable, and feasible in your church context. It is more likely that you will find the ideas from churches in a similar part of the country or churches with a similar demographic to be more helpful or realistic. For example, if your church is located in a small city in Arkansas, the principles and ministry philosophy of the Brooklyn Tabernacle in New York may not be appropriate for your church and may lead to frustration when the same results do not occur. It would be more helpful to investigate and learn from the ministry of a mega-church in Little Rock than from a mega-church in Brooklyn.

It is best to visit churches slightly larger than your own.

Similarly, it is also important to discern what adjustments or modifications must be made to ministry ideas when they are applied in your own church community. Many churches make the mistake of importing new programs or approaches to ministry without accounting for the unique factors or dynamics that influence ministry in their church. For example, one church had not had a lot of experience with small groups, but began to see the value of them for assimilating adults and developing them spiritually. They planned to launch a full-fledged small group ministry, including heavy promotion of small groups, training for small group leaders, and several different small groups for people to choose from. The ministry model they followed seemed to originate in a context similar to theirs, but the small group ministry never caught on.

After much disappointment and discussion, the leaders began to realize that the people in the church were already strongly connected to fellowship groups and classes that met on Sunday morning. Most did not feel the need for more relational connections or spiritual input outside of that weekly commitment. They also discovered that if people did desire more than what was offered on Sunday morning, they networked and launched smaller groups from within their mid-size group. Although launching a small group ministry has been very successful and profitable for many churches, this church already had a strong network of mid-size groups, which diminished the need for people to get involved in new, smaller groups.

Involve New People and Listen to Their Ideas

New worship attendees are probably the best resource you have to generate new ideas and gain fresh perspectives on your ministry. Their input is beneficial for a number of reasons:

- They often ask thoughtful questions without an agenda.
- They are not familiar with the tradition of the church or what is expected.

- They do not have a lot of emotional baggage surrounding the church's ministries.
- They often have recent experience with other ministries.
- They are usually not burnt out from serving.

Churches often overlook new people as a source for ideas, despite the incredible contributions they can make to the ministry. We often write off their observations as uninformed or dismiss their ideas as naïve. It is a travesty that our arrogance prohibits us from capitalizing on this free resource.

> New people are a great source of new ideas. Listen to them!

The perspectives of new attendees can be of great advantage in brainstorming, generating ideas, and planning. So how do we tap into their ideas? How do we attract them to our ministries and make it easy for them to get involved? How can we best utilize the new people God brings to our ministry?

If your ministry or church does not have a lot of new people, you may want to consider doing some things to attract new people to your ministry or increase the ease with which new people can get involved. One college ministry offers freshmen a discount on the ministry's fall retreat as an incentive for new freshman students to attend. By offering a discount to first-time attendees or maybe a discount to certain groups in the church—perhaps young families who are strapped or seniors on a fixed income—you communicate that these people are of value to your ministry.

Involving new people and listening to their ideas requires that you be intentional about seeking them out. There are formal and informal ways to tap into the observations and ideas of people who are new to your church. A more formal approach would be to create a focus group with people who have been at the church less than two years and ask them questions about the issues at hand. This could be done with a large group of fifteen to twenty people or a smaller group of five to ten people.

A more informal approach would be to hang out where new people tend to congregate or where they have gotten involved in your church. How many new people do you know personally? Do you tend to socialize in the same circles that they do? It is crucial that you make an effort to get outside your current relational network and meet new people. For example, if many of the new families in your church began coming through the sports ministries for their children, then attend the sporting events and get to know the parents on the sidelines. If there is an established method of welcoming new people in the church—like a dessert at the pastor's house, a gathering between services, or a newcomers' barbeque—ask if you can attend some of those events. Use that time to get to know some of the new people, listen to their reasons for coming to the church, discover their interests in ministry, and learn about their background or experience at other churches.

Another informal method of gathering feedback and ideas from new people is to simply take them out to coffee and pick their brain. If you notice someone who is getting involved, seems observant, has good people skills, and has already suggested an idea or two, offer to take them out to coffee. The amount of helpful and frank input you receive by doing nothing more than asking good questions will probably surprise you!

You also want to be intentional about incorporating new people into the leadership of your ministry or onto a task group or planning team. They will help to bring balance to the team by offering insights from a slightly different perspective. However, sometimes new people may be hesitant to make a long-term commitment until they feel comfortable with the ministry. Or they may not be in a stage in life where they can make an ongoing commitment to join the leadership of a ministry.

Many parents of young families, for example, may be hesitant to commit to spending another night of the week away from their family even though they are supportive of the ministry and would love to get involved. Instead, you may want to consider inviting them to attend one meeting for the planning team, rather than inviting them to join the team.

Inviting specific people to a planning meeting, without requiring them to commit to an ongoing role, will broaden the spectrum of feedback you get. Sometimes, the people you invite will learn more about the ministry, feel a sense of commitment to it, and begin to increase their involvement. Other times it will give people an opportunity or venue to share ideas that they would not otherwise have given. Offering opportunities for new people to get involved and share ideas without responsibility will expand the pool of ideas you have, as well as helping to identify potential leaders.

Create Time for Your Leaders to Dream Big

Too often we pull people together on a Wednesday night after a long day at work and expect leaders to come up with fresh and creative ideas to plan the future of our church. We hold the meeting in an ugly Sunday school classroom with fluorescent lighting and uncomfortable seating, and then wonder why everyone was restless to wrap up the meeting! We have to remember that our leaders are people, not machines. If we meet on an evening during the workweek, our leaders are probably feeling some residual stress from a busy workday or are thinking about what they need to get done at home before the day is over. If they are leading any ministries or teaching in any capacity, it is likely that they are also concerned about the next meeting they are responsible to run or the next class they are responsible to teach.

What if, rather than squeezing creativity from exhaustion, you pulled these mature and experienced men and women away from the distractions of the day or the pressure of the workweek? What if you spent time brainstorming when the ministry has finished for the year and your leaders were not pressed to lead their next meeting or event? What if you took the group of leaders away for an extended period of brainstorming and praying on a Saturday morning? What if you had the group in an environment that was comfortable and conducive to creativity rather than productivity—a back patio, a living room, the back room at a restaurant, a park, a cabin, or anywhere near water?

When you plan time for your leaders without the pressures of ministry and their own workloads, you will be surprised by the creativity in the group and the openness to ideas and new thinking. One ministry that met weekly during the school year would always schedule a Saturday morning in July to reconnect, welcome new leaders, introduce the theme of the year, brainstorm new ways of doing things, and pray for the year. At the meeting, they did not make a schedule for the year, make any difficult decisions, or delineate responsibilities at this meeting—the focus was helping people get to know one another so they felt comfortable offering their insights and brainstorming together. The meeting was held in someone's home where there was space for them to gather inside and outside, and there was always some sort of food involved.

> Nothing happens unless first a dream.
> —CARL SANDBURG

The staff was always amazed at how creative, flexible, and fun the leadership team could be when pulled away from the pressures of teaching or leading the ministry during the school year. Although some of the ideas and thoughts that came out of those Saturdays in July were too much for the group to implement, many of the ideas could be used and there was a sense of participation and enjoyment of the whole process.

As you think about creating a venue for your ministry to dream big without the pressure of doing ministry, you will want to consider three things:

Timing. Most ministries and churches have certain rhythms. There are times of the year that are busy, and times when things slow down. When is the best time for your team to meet when they are not exhausted or feeling the pressure of the ministry? When is the best time for them to be able to dream big and not immediately deal with the details or difficulties of implementing new ideas?

Location. Most people will feel more comfortable, creative, and relaxed outside of a church building (unless you have an incredible church facility!). Where would be a good place for your team to meet that is comfortable and conducive to interaction?

Length of time. Most people at your church will be working full-time or taking care of children, so it is important to find a time where they do not feel the pressure to wrap up the meeting and head home. Is there a good time on the weekend to meet, like a Saturday morning or a Sunday afternoon, where people can plan to be away for three to four hours?

Remind Them of Their Central Purpose or Key Values

One large church held an annual retreat for over twenty-five years that was relatively well-attended. When a new staff person was hired, she asked the others on staff what the purpose of the retreat was. The question was met with several answers about building relationships, Bible teaching, solitude, worship, rest, encouragement, fun, spiritual growth, and other things. The responses sounded more like the schedule for the weekend than the goals of the weekend. Although the retreat certainly made positive contributions in the lives of those attending, it was clear that there was no central purpose or even key values that were driving the annual retreat. Over the years, the retreat became a staple ministry that included just about everything.

That was fine until attendance started dropping slowly and the leadership wanted to make changes to the retreat. It was very difficult to make any changes, however, because everything seemed important. There was no central purpose to accomplish or key values to define the weekend, so there was no system of discerning what aspects of the retreat were non-negotiable or where resources should be allocated. The team leading the ministry was committed to serving in their areas of responsibility, but they were not united around a common purpose for the retreat.

Sometimes ministries try to accomplish too much considering the time and energy they have. Even when a ministry has a clearly stated purpose, people quickly grow accustomed to the side benefits of the ministry that have developed over the years. The leadership may be able to identify their main purpose, but the team of people who actually run the ministry are often much less attuned to it. Their efforts to serve may be genuine, but they are not coordinated or driven by the central purpose or values of the ministry. They may be overwhelmed by all that needs to get done for the weekend, but they are not willing to let anything go, because it all has some positive value. They may want new energy and life to their ministry, but they are not able to channel their efforts in a single direction.

> Leaders forget the purpose of their ministry in four weeks; participants forget it in two.

Ministries that lack direction need to be recalibrated around their central purpose and key values, so they can focus on the most important and significant contributions of the ministry. If there is no central purpose, leaders need to develop a central purpose, along with the key values to support that purpose. When there is clarity regarding the central purpose of the ministry, the team can direct more energy toward that purpose and have freedom to accomplish the central purpose in the best way possible. This recalibration of ministry frees up resources and energy that had been devoted to maintaining the peripheral aspects of the ministry and releases them to be directed at and improve the other crucial aspects of the ministry. Bringing clarity, definition, and attention to the central purpose of your ministry can actually bring greater creativity and effectiveness to your ministry.

Making innovative changes in your ministry is not easy, but it can be done. It is necessary in order to improve the quality of your ministry and respond to the changing dynamics of your community and our culture. I hope you are encouraged by the simple suggestions mentioned in this chapter to help you generate ideas and be innovative in ministry, no matter what the size or age of your church. May you embrace the opportunity for growth and effectiveness that change brings.

HOW TO STAY OUT OF A RUT

How do we keep from getting stuck in a rut? Here are some tips to keep your ministries fresh and nurture a culture of innovation.

1. Try something new each year in your ministry.

Tell your leaders that you expect them to try five new things this year *and* that you expect them to fail at three of them. Trying out a new ministry is really not a failure, but an experiment that teaches us new ways to serving others.

2. Involve new people in the leadership of your ministries.

Encourage your leaders to keep their eye out for new people and to recruit them for their ministries, and praise your leaders when they do. New people bring fresh ideas and insights to bear on old problems that are worth listening to and using.

3. Share new ideas that have worked.

Often, ministries in large churches are so "siloed" that they do not learn from each other. However, other ministries could benefit from them because they work in the same church, generally serve the same population, have learned to work with the same resources, or developed helpful practices and systems.

4. Dedicate time for your church staff and volunteer leaders to meet together.

Discuss challenges or problems each of the ministries face and offer ideas and solutions for respective ministries. The staff and leaders in small churches may not have the luxury of many team members or other staff to bounce ideas off of, so taking time together to talk about each ministry may help identify some very simple but effective solutions.

5. Develop a sister relationship with another church or church ministry.

People have relationships or natural networks in other churches. These connections can be nurtured, and both churches can benefit from one another. Denominational connections can be helpful, but a sister church relationship does not have to be doctrinally based. It can be more informal and centered on ministry development rather than theological compatibility.

MY PLANNING NOTEBOOK

Five ways to foster creativity:

- Create dissonance through exposure to other ministries.

My Comments:

- Investigate the ministries of churches slightly larger than ours.

My Comments:

- Involve new people and listen to their ideas.

My Comments:

- Create the time and space for leaders to dream.

My Comments:

- Remind leaders of the purpose of their ministries.

There is nothing more difficult to take in hand, more
perilous to conduct, or more uncertain in its success,
than to take the lead in the introduction of a new
order of things.

—NICCOLÒ MACHIAVELLI

NINE

Plan for Change

A number of years ago, Alvin Toffler coined the term *future shock* to describe the inability of people to cope with rapid change in society. Throughout history, there has always been change. The difference today is how fast change is taking place. What once took years or decades to change now happens in a few months. Heraclitus's famous statement appears to be truer than ever: "There is nothing permanent except change."

A Brief History of Change in the Church

Major historical events in the history of the Church illustrate how the pace of change is increasing. For example, after the fall of Rome in A.D. 476, the Western world entered into a period called the Dark Ages. This era lasted roughly one thousand years until the Protestant Reformation began in 1517. Changes occurred throughout this lengthy period of time but at such a slow pace that people hardly paid any attention. During the 1500s, great change took place in a relatively short period of time as Martin Luther, John Calvin, Urlich Zwingli, and other reformers focused attention on the excesses of the Roman Church.

After the Reformation, events appeared to settle down until the Great Awakening began in the United Kingdom and its North American colonies in the 1730s and 1740s. John and Charles Wesley, George Whitefield, and Jonathan Edwards spearheaded a movement that brought extensive change to Christianity. New ideals on holiness, conversion, and worship were introduced that are still observed in our churches today.

About one hundred years later, in the 1830s, a Second Great Awakening occurred that again brought change to the Church in the form of evangelicalism, revivalism, and personal piety. Dwight L. Moody and Charles Haddon Spurgeon stressed the importance of personal faith in Christ so effectively that they forged the first mega-churches of the modern era.

Following the deaths of Moody and Spurgeon, churches settled into a more leisurely pace that was interrupted by two world wars in the first half of the 1900s. But a mere fifty years later, with World War II behind, great change once again swept through the Church. Major shifts regarding worship, theology, and mission overwhelmed churches, as fresh insights on the Holy Spirit, spiritual gifts, lay ministry, and the Church in general worked their way into the thinking of church leaders.

The point in looking at this brief overview of Church history is to show that the pace of major change is occurring in an ever-shortening space of time. It took one thousand years from the fall of Rome for the Protestant Reformation to jolt the Church. Yet, it was only two hundred years until the First Great Awakening, then one hundred years to the Second Great Awakening, then around fifty years to the evangelical movement in the latter half of the 1900s. Today, the shelf life of any Church movement seems to last around fifteen years and appears to be getting shorter.

Channels of Change

All life depends on change. Indeed if there is no change, there is no life. Look at the contrast between the Sea of Galilee and the Dead Sea in Israel. The Sea of Galilee is alive with an abundance of fish, because the Jordan River flows into and out of it. The constantly changing water revives the sea, so new life can produce and thrive. Not so with the Dead Sea. The Jordan River flows into it, but not out of it. It has no marine vegetation, no fish, and no life.

The same pattern is observed in all living organisms, including churches. As someone once said, "When you're through changing, you're dead." Life is found in churches that are willing to change, but unhealthy churches are often the ones unwilling to make appropriate changes. Effective church leaders recognize, not only that change is here to stay, but also that change is necessary if our churches are to remain healthy and vibrant families of faith. My observations over the last quarter century lead me to believe that change takes place through four different channels.

Revival

First, change takes place through revival. Revival happens as God's people pray for change, especially change in the spiritual condition of their church. I remember working with a church in the Northwest that shared a wonderful story of revival. A small group of faithful people prayed for ten years that God would bring a fresh spirit to the church, and he did! After a decade of prayer, God brought a warm renewal of spiritual life, as church members released old hurts, newcomers came to faith in Christ, and the church grew from fewer than one hundred people to more than eight hundred in a few short years.

Disruption

Second, change takes place through major disruptions. A pastor of a church in Northern California called me a few years ago in late November to tell me that the church he served had burned down on Thanksgiving Day. Far from being a disaster, this event proved to be a blessing. Since the church could not meet in its sanctuary, it held worship services in the gym. Since they could not use the organ, they used guitars, drums, and an electric keyboard. Since they could no longer meet in one service, they started a second worship service. All these changes brought a new spirit of life and vitality to the church, and it all started due to the major disruption caused by a fire.

> Major changes in a church come via revival, disruption, pastoral moves, and planning.

New Pastor

Third, major changes take place with the arrival of a new pastor. Few pastors accept an appointment or call to a church unless they sense some potential or vision for the church. By combining new vision with a fresh voice and the typical honeymoon period of a new pastorate, changes take place with relative ease. Sometimes the initial period of a new pastor's ministry creates enough changes that churches explode with new energy. One church in Wyoming called a new pastor to replace a retiring pastor who had served the church for twenty-five years. The last few years of the older, beloved pastor's ministry were ones of decline as he coasted into retirement. When the new pastor arrived, the church was ready for change, and the new pastor hit the ground running and making significant changes that resuscitated an otherwise stale church.

Planning

These three means of bringing change to a church are real, but the fourth and primary way change comes to a church is through planning. Some changes take place naturally. Carpets wear out and are replaced. Paint peels and is repainted. Grass dies and is replanted. But, a major change of ministry direction normally requires planning. Some time ago I consulted with a church in Michigan. Due to cutbacks in the local industry, the town around the church suffered decline as jobs became scarce. Rather than take a reactive stance to the crisis, the church chose to take a proactive position. A planning team was formed, research was conducted to determine needs in the community that the church could address, and a plan was designed and put into practice. Over the next few years, every church in the town lost members and worshipers. The lone exception was this church with a plan. A well-designed plan is the main way to bring about change to a church. So, let us not just acknowledge the fact of change, but be agents of change in our churches by developing a plan for the future.

Principles of Change

It may come as a surprise to some people, but Jesus was a change agent. Eating with tax collectors, touching lepers, eating and drinking when others felt he should be fasting and praying—all these actions were changes that brought criticism to Jesus and his disciples. Jesus responded to this criticism by saying,

No one tears a piece of cloth from a new garment and puts it on an old garment; otherwise he will both tear the new, and the piece from the new will not match the old. And no one puts new wine into old wineskins; otherwise the new wine will burst the skins and it will be spilled out, and the skins will be ruined. But new wine must be put into fresh wineskins. And no one, after drinking old wine wishes for new; for he says, "The old is good enough." (Luke 5:36–39)

There is a paradox in the midst of rapid change. The more things change the more people look for places of stability. A friend once remarked to me, "I'm surrounded by changes wherever I turn. The one place where I find stability is my church. I don't want it to change." Like my friend, many people fear change, cling to the familiar, and draw security from the tradition and customary practices found in their church. They want things to stay the same, to keep the *status quo*. If church leaders do not conform to the normal customs and practices of the church, some people will be upset. If they advocate change, they will face the scrutiny of some and the wrath of others.

Jesus was an agent of change. Yet, at the same time, "Jesus Christ is the same yesterday and today and forever" (Heb. 13:8 NIV). Jesus did not change everything, but from the beginning, he refused to conform to Pharisaic practices that placed people under an unnecessary burden or distorted the law or was contrary to the will of God.

Most likely, the changes you are hoping to bring about are due to a desire to restore health and vitality to your church. My good friend, Neil Anderson, offers the following four principles for understanding when change is appropriate in a church.[1]

Changes Should Be Appropriate for the Situation
Jesus neither condemns nor condones John's disciples and their desire to fast. "It is OK for them to fast; it is OK if mine do not" was the perspective of Jesus. Jesus' point was that it was not appropriate for his disciples to fast while he was with them. The day would come when he would go away, then they would fast.

It is not a question of ritual, but rather a question of purpose. Appropriateness requires an answer to the question, Why? The reason, "We have always done it this way before," is unacceptable. Christian practices often continue for years, outliving their purpose, until someone asks, "Why are we still doing this?" If you verbalize the question, then watch the defenses come up!

Changes should be appropriate to the church's situation.

Many evangelical churches have multiple services during the week, but few remember why. Originally, Sunday morning was for instruction and worship, Sunday evening was for evangelism, and Wednesday evening was for prayer. Virtually no churches do it that way any more. Evangelism (if there is an evangelistic service) has moved to the Sunday morning seeker service. On Sunday evening, some churches focus on body life, some do an informal repeat of the morning service, and others have done away with services altogether. Most churches stopped using Wednesday evening for a prayer service long ago. Few people know or remember why they have an adult fellowship group. Consequently, most groups never fulfill the greatest purpose for which they exist, which is to provide the fellowship base for incorporating new people into the church and meeting one another's needs.

The greatest avenue for change is to clarify the mission of all existing ministries or groups. I sat with the leaders of an adult group about two years ago and helped them hammer out a mission statement. Through this clarification process, some major changes took place in their church. Within two years, the church had doubled. Asking *why* forced them to evaluate their purpose and ministry, and necessary changes came.

Change Should Be Consistent with the Inward Condition of the Heart

Holding on to external forms and habits that no longer correlate to the heart is repugnant to God. Jesus railed against praying in vain repetitions and putting on gloomy faces while fasting. Consistency cries for an affirmative answer to the question, "Is it real?"

The Christian community searches for truth, while the world searches for reality. The two concepts overlap, but I am convinced we must be real in order to be right. Change is most needed when Christians sit stoically week after week reciting endless creeds in utter hypocrisy. Tragically, such Christians are the most resistant to change, because they have not continued to grow under the instruction of the Word. Many people come to church to fulfill a religious obligation rather than coming to the changeless Christ and saying, "Change me in order that I may be like you." Paradoxically, the ones who have a real Christian experience are the ones who are free to change their Christian practices because they are committed to the substance of their faith, not the form.

Form always follows function, but people have a tendency to fixate on the form. The key to change is to focus on the heart as Jesus did. Organizational renewal will not bring spiritual renewal. When the spiritual tide is out, every little tadpole wants his own tide pool to swim in. But when the spiritual tide is in, it becomes like one big ocean and the fish swim as though someone is synchronizing every move. When the Spirit is in charge, almost any organization will work, but when he is not, then the best program and organization will not work either. It must be real or it will not work.

The Forms of Our Christian Practice Must Change

Here the Lord carefully chose his metaphors. The garment and the wineskins are the external dress and the container, not the substance of our faith. They represent the religious customs and practices, the traditions, the forms, which the substance is packaged in. The point is the garment needs mending, and the wineskin is old! What worked before is not working anymore. Times change, culture changes, and what worked twenty years ago may not work today. What does not change is the object of our faith. The problem is that time honored faith and long established practice begins to blend together and become indistinguishable. When a person advocates a different form or practice, it becomes readily apparent that people's security is tied in with the long established practice instead of the time-honored faith.

The reasoning behind the resistance seems logical: "I came to Christ singing that song," or "It worked for me; I don't see why it won't work for my children." I have sat in worship services all choked up, listening to music or a favorite passage and was surprised that it did not have the same impact on my children. The questions we must continually ask are, "Is it relevant?" and "Does it relate?" This is the most difficult struggle for church leadership today.

This problem is not spiritual. It is sociological. Why is it that a good Bible-believing church that faithfully carries out its ministry struggles to hold onto its young people, while another church down the block rents a store building and has four times more kids in a matter of months? We must continuously ask, "Does it relate?" That leads us to the next principle.

Changes Should Preserve the Old and the New Wine

The old wine is vastly superior to the new. But many eulogize the venerable past and love to contrast it with the present. Make no mistake; the old is often perceived as wise, gentle, reverent, and good. Because of the quality of its vintage, there is a strong prejudice against any proposed change. Even Jesus concedes to loving the old wine of Jewish piety: "And no one, after drinking the old wine wishes for new; for he says, 'The old is good enough'" (Luke 5:39). But its supply will run out!

On the other hand, the new wine may at times be bitter and harsh, but can we object to its existence? Can we deny the need for new forms of style—especially music, art, and even instruction? We may not desire it, because it is strange and novel, but wisdom says not to spurn, spill, or spoil it. This last principle asks the question, "Does it unify?" The unity of the Spirit is already present; our task is to instruct the church that all are responsible to practice unity, by tolerating another person's preference and accepting the diversity of the body as a good thing. The task is difficult, but not impossible. If we are to accomplish our purpose, we must ask why we are doing what we are doing. Is it real? Does it relate? Does it unify?

How Is Change Brought About?

Spiritual leaders need to be constantly aware that people are prone to associate practice with principle. The leader who is constantly presenting new ideas and changing practices without a well thought-out strategy is tampering with people's sense of security and balance. People are most comfortable in the status quo and naturally resist any change. Therefore, the leader must carefully weigh every proposed change and proceed with the wisdom of God. Our goal is to reduce stress and remove burdens, not add to them! What follows is a suggested strategy for change that starts with asking the right questions and ends with understanding resistance.

Questions to Ask

There are several questions that should be considered before a proposed change is implemented.

What are the relative advantages? It is essential to determine how people perceive the need for change. Most people reason, "If it isn't broke, don't fix it." If the resistance clearly outweighs the need for change, then the leader better wait.

Another colloquial concept is, "You cannot move any faster than you can educate." If the change really is advantageous, then the leader must make others aware of the relative need. The biggest error made at this stage is to attack what is rather than extol the virtues of what could be. Never try to take a bone away from a dog; you will only have a fight. Throw the dog a steak, and he will voluntarily spit the bone out.

What will be the social or relational impact? People develop a sense of ownership and assume a certain amount of status in any ministry or working relationship. If a proposed change will diminish someone's status or threaten ownership, there will be resistance. As much as possible, discern the potential impact beforehand, because it will significantly determine the proposed strategy. In a ministry where fellowship is essential, leaders must consider the priority of relationships. As a general rule, any move forward at the cost of fellowship, the price is too high! We must be diligent to preserve the unity of the spirit (Eph. 4:3). Likewise, we must obey the first and second Great Commandments, which are to love God and our fellow man, because on these two commandments depend the whole Law and the Prophets (Matt. 22:37–40). It is never right to violate the fruit of the Spirit in the name of progress. If it cannot be done in love, then it should not be done at all. The only exceptions are those modeled by Christ.

Is the proposed change divisible? As a general rule, massive changes are harder to pull off and meet more resistance than smaller changes brought about in incremental steps. Patience should be exercised if something can be done in parts. The visionary leader must see the bigger picture, but the implementation is usually done better in parts. Each part contributes to the success of the whole. This is probably what Isaiah had in mind when he said that "vigorous young men stumble badly, Yet those who wait for the LORD Will gain new strength (Isa. 40:30–31). Patience is a prerequisite to change.

Is it reversible? If people know that they can always go back to the old way, they will be less resistant. The hardest change to implement is change that is irreversible. If it cannot be reversed, the perceived risk must be minimized. Leadership will never be under more intense scrutiny than when they propose irreversible change. Many see Moses as the greatest Old Testament leader because of the magnitude of the task of leading the people out of Egypt, but we also need to remember how often his leadership was contested to the point that God had to intervene. Crossing the Red Sea and the Jordan River required exceptional godly leadership. The Israelites expressed it well when speaking to Joshua, Moses' successor: "Just as we obeyed Moses in all things, so we will obey you; only may the LORD your God be with you as He was with Moses" (Josh. 1:17).

Is it compatible? Does it fit? One of the most common mistakes leaders make is to assume that a program working well in one place will work in their ministry. Not necessarily so. Principles are transferable; programs may not be. Every leader must adapt his or her leadership style to the people he or she is leading. In the same way, programs must be tailored to each situation.

Is it communicable? Can it be clearly explained to all involved? If it cannot, the leadership is saying, "Trust me." The congregation may say, "Go ahead," but it is a blind obedience that seldom comes with any sense of ownership or true commitment. Effective leaders share a vision that people can clearly see and understand. As a general rule, the average person should be able to explain and defend the proposed change. Remember: The more complex the change, the greater the resistance.

How much commitment is required? How much time will it take? How much commitment is required of the people in terms of money, time, and energy? Are they willing to make the commitment? This has to be learned beforehand. Counting the cost is equated with true discipleship (Luke 14:28–35).

There is definitely a need for new wineskins. There is an even greater need for leaders that are "wise as serpents and harmless as doves." More often than not, Christian churches and organizations are prepared to go beyond the place where present leaders have taken them. May God enable us to provide the type of leadership that will accomplish his purpose in his time.

ONE PASTOR'S STORY OF CHANGE

A decade ago, I struggled through a class on change theory. The major class project was to analyze the process of change that we were presently going through in our respective organizations. I chronicled the events that had taken place in our church over the past couple of years.

I began my ministry with the mutual understanding that we would develop a new form of church government. Other candidates had questioned the church's organizational structure, which consisted of four independent boards. Many of the charter members were still attending, and they held most of the leadership positions. The unity they had at the beginning was no longer there, because the personnel on the boards had changed during the years and there was nothing organizational to tie the church together. They were aware of the problem and agreed to restructure the government with my guidance. In six months, we had established a single board system and changed significantly the constitution of the church.

Concurrent with that change, an opportunity presented itself to sell the property that the charter members had pieced together and purchase new property. The new location was vastly superior to the old property. The people who had put together the first constitution and had worked so hard buying the first property were the big majority on the board of the church.

To add to the picture, significant change was taking place in the style of ministry. I tend to be an open and informal leader and the previous pastor was a perfectionist and quite formal. It was most evident in worship. I believe worship is a joyful celebration with uplifting music and congregational sharing. The first pastor preferred solemn assemblies!

I was experiencing a lot of resistance that I was having a hard time accepting. Everyone agreed that the new government and constitution was better and the new property was a gift from God. The majority of people loved the freedom in our worship services. So why the resistance? I'm sure that some of it was personality, but generally speaking, when one doesn't conform to the customs and practices of the established norm, the establishment will be offended. Tradition and custom are gods to the status quo. If you advocate or practice differently, you will come under the scrutiny of some and the wrath of others. I was taking the first steps in the process of change, which are by far the most perilous.

Since that first experience of being a pastoral change agent, I have learned a few things. Recently I had the privilege to lead an established church through a constitutional change that reorganized from twenty-six committees to seven. The pastor had been there for thirty years and the church had grown from nothing to over one thousand attendees. However, the organization had developed with little planning or purpose. Amazingly, this change took place without any dissention. The major keys were the credibility of the pastor and the wise use of some biblical principles that Jesus taught and modeled for changing established practices.

—Author Unknown

MY PLANNING NOTEBOOK

Insights on change:

- The only constant today is change.

My Comments:

- The shelf life of a ministry in today's church is between five and fifteen years.

My Comments:

- Changes take place through four means: revival, disruption, pastoral moves, and planning.

My Comments:

- Changes should be appropriate to our situation, consistent with God's heart, relevant to our times, and preserve both the old and new wine.

My Comments:

- The best changes are well planned.

NOTE

1. Portions of this chapter were written by Neil Anderson for a class we taught together titled "Biblical Leadership and Management" at Talbot School of Theology, La Mirada, California.

The church exists by mission,
as fire exists by burning.

—EMIL BRUNNER

TEN

What We Do: Mission

When you hear words like *purpose, mission, values, objectives, intent, aim, target, ends, means,* and *goals,* what do you think? How do you feel? If you are like many people, these words are confusing. For instance, what is the difference between mission and purpose? How comparable are objectives and goals? Does it really matter anyway? For others, any mention of these terms causes their eyes to glaze over in boredom.

Some leaders have stressed the narrowest of differences in terminology to the point that confusion reigns in all but their own minds, but such does not need to be the case. There is a simple way to plan the future of your church that works and is not confusing or boring.

An excellent comprehensive plan is comprised of four strategic statements that serve to define a church's direction. I like to state the four aspects of a plan this way:

- Mission: What we do
- Vision: What we see
- Values: What we believe
- Goals: What we achieve

Let's take them one by one.

Mission is sometimes referred to as *purpose*. It does not matter which word you use, as long as you are consistent in using the same word. Mission is the biblical reason a church exists. As such, the mission of a church never changes, and it can never be completely accomplished. For example, here is how one church states its mission: The mission of Grace Church is to present the Gospel to all people preparing them to be followers of Jesus Christ.

Attributes of a Church Mission Statement

As long as there are people living without a personal relationship with Christ and others who need to grow in their walk with Christ, the mission of Grace Church will still be viable. A church's mission is the most stable part of its strategic statements. It may be helpful to illustrate this by thinking of a hot air balloon (see figure below). The basket on a hot air balloon is the part that is most stable. Normally made in the form of a wicker basket, the basket retains its shape at all times, while the balloon and ties can be collapsed.

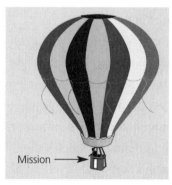

In a similar fashion, a church's mission statement serves as the firm foundation from which the other three strategic statements ascend. Thus, a mission statement must have at least three attributes.

Biblical

First, a mission statement must be biblical; that is, it must be founded on the Word of God. The mission statement above is supported by the Great Commission in Matthew 28:19–20:

> Go therefore and make disciples of all nations, baptizing them in the name of the Father and the Son and the Holy Spirit, teaching them to observe all that I commanded you; and lo, I am with you always, even to the end of the age.

Other supporting verses could be added to show the concept of a mission statement arises from Scripture, but the Great Commission is a commonly used Scripture from which many churches form a mission statement.

Thematic

Second, it must state the big ideas or themes of Scripture rather than what programs a church offers. Mission is not a list of a church's programs, but a statement of the purpose of the programs. While the first statements are often found in actual mission statements, a church would do well to change the first statements below to the following ones:

- *From* offering Sunday school *to* educating children
- *From* offering vacation Bible school *to* evangelizing children
- *From* offering adult Bible fellowships *to* discipling adults
- *From* offering counseling *to* caring for hurting people

None of the first statements are necessarily wrong, but they focus on specific programs rather than identifying the underlying purpose, as the second ones do. Look again at the mission statement above. Grace Church's basic mission is to prepare people to be followers of Jesus Christ. That statement focuses on people's need to walk with God. Note that nothing in the statement says how this mission will be accomplished. It does not list anything that even remotely sounds like a program or ministry—and that is the way a mission should be.

Memorable

Third, a mission statement must be short and easy to remember! In most cases, a church's mission statement should be less than twenty-five words in length. The previous example is only twenty-one words, and it could even be shortened to fifteen words: The mission of Grace Church is to prepare people to be followers of Jesus Christ. Long mission statements are notoriously difficult to keep in mind.

Now, some might say it seems too short to be helpful. So, at Grace they have developed three basic versions of their mission statement: a short, a standard, and an expanded version.

Short Version: The mission of Grace Church is to prepare people to be followers of Jesus Christ.

Standard Version: The mission of Grace Church is to present Christ to all people and prepare them to be followers of Jesus Christ.

Expanded Version: The mission of Grace Church is to *present* Christ to people in a

- Creative—using new, innovative methods
- Compelling—in the power of the Holy Spirit
- Caring—within sensitive, compassionate relationships

way and to *prepare* them to be followers of Jesus Christ who are:

- Committed to the Word—growing in maturity
- Committed to Serve—giving in time, talent, and treasure
- Committed to Others—caring for one another.

It is very difficult to get the entire congregation to remember anything but the shorter version. The expanded version is more like the church's philosophy of ministry, since it tells more about the thinking behind the church's approach. For example, this church's philosophy is to use new, innovative methods.

Discovering Your Church's Mission

So how does your congregation arrive at a mission statement? First, start with your pastor and allow him or her to write the original version. Then pass it around to other leaders and take suggestions on how to revise the statement. Eventually share it with most or all the congregation to see what they might add. Developing a mission statement in this manner is called pulsing. The idea is derived from the concept of taking a church's pulse. In diagram form it looks like this.

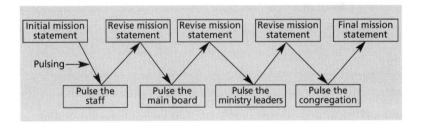

Each step takes an ever-widening pulse of the leaders and people of the church. The advantage is that everyone in the church is given an opportunity to contribute to the formation of the mission statement. By the time a church goes through the pulsing process, there is solid ownership of the mission statement among the people.

As you develop your mission statement, keep in mind two very important ideas. First, mission is not about us; it is about them.

I do not know if it is true, but there is a maxim in big-game hunting that states that the larger an animal is, the harder it is to see. Evidently, the animal is so obvious that it is mistaken for something so benign and familiar that it is missed. The point? We sometimes miss the obvious. It is something like the old adage: "You can't see the forest for the trees." We spend a great deal of time missing the obvious. Jesus clearly said, "For the Son of Man has come to seek and to save that which was lost" (Luke 19:10). Since Jesus is the head of the Church, it seems pretty clear that the mission of a local church must reflect his concern for the lost. If church leaders would just take Christ's commands to the Church seriously from the beginning, they could arrive at a mission statement more quickly.

Second, there is a big difference between having a shared mission and merely having something in common.

At first, pastors preach about the mission statement from the pulpit and hope people catch the spirit of it. Later they discover that people cannot even recall having heard it. It is important to communicate your mission in at least five different ways. This can be done by hanging banners in your auditorium that proclaim the mission statement or printing it on all pieces of literature from the church. It must be on your business cards, letterhead, and envelopes. The pastor should weave it into sermons about every other week so that people will remember it. In short, do all you can to keep your mission before the people. As you consistently share the mission with the congregation over about a five year period of time, it will finally get into their minds and hearts.

Communicating Your Church's Mission

Most church leaders are surprised at how long it takes for people to remember their mission. You see the problem is not just getting people to remember the mission statement; it is getting them to own it! Your people have a lot in common, but getting them to have a shared mission means going to a higher level. A good illustration of what you are trying to develop is seen in the early church in Jerusalem. Two times it is said of the first church that they had "one mind" (Acts 1:14; 2:46), and once it is said that they were of "one heart and soul" (Acts 4:32). We want our people to be of one soul, one heart, and one mind when it comes to the mission statement.

Writing a mission statement is no quick fix. There are likely a lot of different reasons why it takes so long for people to remember and own the mission, but part of the problem is the large amount of information that bombards people today. People are literally inundated with input from all directions. Some say we have thousands of messages sent to us each day through radio, TV, Internet, cell phones, e-mails, tweets (Twitter), or conversations for example. Fortunately, God has built filters into our minds that keep most of this information out. It takes repetition to overcome the natural barriers.

Another reason is that the natural process of communication creates loss at every level on the communication chain. Note the following chart.

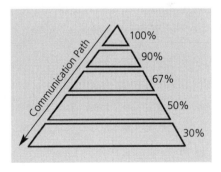

At the top level, the mission is shared with an expectation that the people will remember 100 percent of it. But, as you can see, the second level of leadership actually catches only about 90 percent of it. As the mission is communicated further down the various levels of church leadership, more of it is lost until fewer people understand it. At the third tier of leadership, only about 67 percent of the message is heard. The fourth tier receives only 50 percent. When the communication reaches the congregation, only about 30 percent of the message is received. This is why it takes repetition of the mission for good communication to take. Each time it is shared, more of the message is remembered.

Have you ever played a game at a party where a person whispers something in the ear of a second person? The message is then whispered in the ear of a third person and so forth until it gets to the last person. When the last person receives the message, he or she shares it with the rest of the group. And the message is never the same as it was at first. For some reason, when a message is passed along, a certain percentage is lost in the translation. The farther along the message is passed, the larger a percentage is lost.

Observe how commercials on television or the radio are repeated over and over. The first time you hear a commercial for a fast food restaurant, for instance, you do not remember much about it. But by the time you have heard the commercial repeatedly, you are singing the song. The point is that a church and its leaders must communicate its mission over and over until the people are singing it.

MY PLANNING NOTEBOOK

What we do: Mission

- Mission is the biblical reason our church exists.

My Comments:

- A mission statement should be less than twenty-five words.

My Comments:

- Our mission statement must be communicated to the congregation five different ways.

My Comments:

- Our mission statement must be communicated until people remember it like a fast-food jingle.

My Comments:

- Mission isn't as much about the people in our church as it is about the people outside our church.

You must scale the mountain if you would view the plain.

—CHINESE PROVERB

ELEVEN

What We See: Vision

A legend I heard many years ago illustrates the importance of vision. Once upon a time there lived a king who was growing old. He knew the time was coming when he would need to give the rule of his kingdom to one of his four sons. The question was to which son should he give his kingdom? To answer that question, the king called his four sons together and gave them a challenge.

"I want each of you to go on a long journey," the king said. "While you are on your journey, look for a gift to bring me that will be worthy of my kingdom. Whoever brings me the best gift will receive my kingdom."

Taking up the challenge, the first son left on his journey. After awhile, he came to the Impenetrable Forest. He spent a long time looking for a way through the forest, but could never find a way. However, while looking at one of the trees, he noticed one of the limbs was twisted in an unusual manner. He decided to cut down that branch and make it into a cane for his father. "Surely, this will be a gift worthy of a kingdom," he thought.

The second son also began his journey. He too came to the Impenetrable Forest, but somehow found a way through. Further on, he arrived at the Uncrossable River. After spending some time attempting to ford the river, he gave up. By chance, he peered into the river and noticed a sparkling stone. Reaching into the river to retrieve the stone, he realized that he had found a valuable gem. "Surely this will be a gift worthy of a kingdom," he thought.

Eventually the third son started on his journey. He too came to the Impenetrable Forest and found a way through. He came to the Uncrossable River and found a way across. Then he came to the Unclimbable Mountain. He walked around the base of the mountain looking for a way to the top, but never found a path. While looking for a path up the mountain, he noticed some flowers, the likes of which he had never seen before. He decided to bundle the roots of the flowers and take them back to make a beautiful flower garden for his father. "Surely this will be a gift worthy of a kingdom," he thought.

The fourth son soon began the journey and, like the others, came to the Impenetrable Forest, the Uncrossable River, and the Unclimbable Mountain. He found a way through the forest, over the river, and up to the top of the mountain. As he stood on the top of the mountain, he looked on the other side and saw a luscious, green valley with streams of crystal clear water. The one thing he could not find, however, was a gift for his father that would be worthy of a kingdom. Sadly, he returned to his father's village.

After the sons returned, they presented their father with the gifts they hoped would be worthy of a kingdom. The last son had no gift to give but told his father of the green valley on the other side of the mountain with the crystal clear water.

The following day the father called his sons together. He thanked the first three sons for their gifts, but to the fourth son he gave his kingdom.

> The greatest leadership gift of all is the gift of vision.

Why did he give the fourth son the kingdom? The fourth son gave his father the greatest gift of all—the gift of vision. The father realized that his fourth son had given him a vision of a better future for his people. Perhaps the fourth son could lead the people of the kingdom to the green valley with crystal clear water where they would experience a better life.

A Leader's Job

True leadership is not about managing people; it is about inspiring them. It is vision that inspires, not mission. The job of all leaders is to expand the visionary horizons of their people. The way to do that is to envision a better future, like the fourth son in the story, and lead people in that direction.

> Mission tells us what we do, but vision helps us see it.

One of the biggest mistakes church leaders make is to think that once they have developed a mission statement and communicated it to their people, all their problems are solved. Unfortunately, as important as the mission statement is, it will not energize the church. Only the vision can do that. Mission tells the beginning of things: what we are to do. Vision tells the end of things: where we are going. Let me explain it this way.

Like most people, my wife and I have bills we must pay each month. We save our money and pay our bills, but it is not very exciting to do it. In contrast, a few years ago we dreamed of taking a vacation trip to Hawaii with some close friends. After talking it over with our friends, we decided to go for it, set a date about two years away, and began saving our money for our dream vacation. We saved our money to pay for our dream vacation and enjoyed doing it.

Perhaps you have experienced the joy of saving for a trip or some new item. It is fun to save for a dream, isn't it? The point I am trying to make is this: Mission is like saving money to pay bills. It is something we need to do, but it is not always that exciting. Vision is like saving money for a dream vacation. It is something we find exciting to do.

Look at it this way. Mission tells us *why*; vision tells us *what* and *where*. In one church I attended some years ago, the pastor preached regularly on the mission statement. People actually understood it fairly well. They understood *why* we were a church. However, people did not get involved, few were giving regularly to the offering, and the general morale was low. The problem was they did not understand *what* the church was going to do or *where* it was headed.

Mission proclamations are normally solid statements of biblical truth. Unfortunately, they pack little energy, because mission statements do not call us to do anything specific. Remember, nothing becomes dynamic until it becomes specific.

Imagine yourself sitting in a congregation when the pastor preaches on the mission statement. As the message concludes, the pastor gives an invitation for people in the congregation to make commitments, saying something like, "God calls you to make a commitment of your time, money, and energy to help fulfill our mission. Why not make a personal commitment today?" What are you thinking as you sit in the congregation? Even though you might agree with the mission statement, you would not know to what ministry or program you were committing. Thus, you would be asking the question, "Give my time, money, and energy to what?" Energy comes from knowing specifically what we will be doing to fulfill our mission, as well as where we are headed.

What if the pastor painted a picture of an exciting vision for you? For instance, the pastor might say something like this:

You all know our mission is to present the Gospel to all people. Today, I want to share with you a vision of how we are going to reach people right here in our own city. We have acquired a new video on the life of Jesus that has proven to be effective in reaching people. The video has been field tested in other cities similar to ours, and we feel it will be an excellent tool for us to use in reaching people in our city for Christ. Our vision is to place a copy of this video in every home in our city within the next two years. Yes, this is a big challenge, and we need all of you to take part in fulfilling this vision for it to happen. "What can I do?" you ask. I am glad you asked that question. The videos cost one dollar fifty cents per piece, and we will need twelve thousand videos at a total cost of eighteen thousand dollars. Perhaps some of you could give financially toward the purchase of these videos. We will also need one hundred fifty people to dedicate themselves to delivering one video a week for forty weeks for the next two years. Perhaps you could volunteer to deliver some videos to your neighbors. In addition, we need one hundred prayer intercessors to pray one hour a week for the homes receiving the videos. Perhaps you could join a prayer intercession team.

Notice the difference between the vision and the mission? In this second example, the pastor painted a picture of a vision to help the people see what they were being asked to commit themselves to. It is the vision that creates the lift to get the church moving in a new direction, adding the following to the hot air balloon diagram.

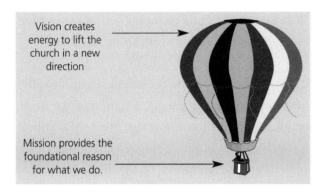

Vision creates energy to lift the church in a new direction

Mission provides the foundational reason for what we do.

The key to empowering a church in a new direction is having a powerful vision that attracts the big three: time, talent, and treasure. Remember, people commit to vision, not to mission.

Discovering God's Vision for Your Church

Scripture demonstrates that God gives his vision to a single person who then is given the responsibility to share it with others. Think of God's vision given to Abram (Gen. 12), Joseph (Gen. 37), Nehemiah (Neh. 1), Peter (Acts 10), Paul (Acts 9), and others throughout Scripture. Other people help to refine and shape the final version of the vision statement itself, but the original vision normally comes through one individual. Rest assured, boards and committees may be good at discussion and decision-making, but rarely are they visionary.

Developing a vision usually takes six steps, although it does not always work out in a one, two, three fashion.

Pray

First, pray and ask God to show you his vision for your local church. God has placed your congregation in this time and place for a reason. He not only has a wonderful plan for your life, but for your church too. Ask him to reveal his vision to you and your church.

Make a List

Second, make a long written list of what you sense God wants your church to do in the next five to ten years. Look at your church as part of a larger picture. How does it fit into the social structure of your community? Your city? Your state? Your nation? Your world? How might any of these areas be different because your church is there? How might your church touch the lives, the hearts, and the souls of people in your community?

After making your list, sift through it several times, each time striking out the weaker ideas. Run some of your thoughts by trusted colleagues or leaders to see what they are sensing God wants to do through your church. As your list grows smaller, you will find that the value remaining grows greater.

Write It Down

Third, write down your vision. Make a habit of thinking about your church's vision. As you think, write your thoughts in graphic detail, visualizing what you see happening in the future of your church.

- Write it purposefully—why is your vision important?
- Write it precisely—what do you see taking place?
- Write it pictorially—what will the end result look like?

Share your written ideas with others around you, listening to their comments and suggestions, and then making revisions on your vision.

Read It

Fourth, read your vision every day. Begin the first steps to communicate the vision to your church leaders. Pulse the church on your vision until it becomes clear in your mind, as well as in others in the congregation. Believe your vision will happen.

Communicate

Fifth, communicate your vision in multiple ways—pulpit, personal conversations, e-mails, written letters, banners, at leadership retreats, articles in church newsletters or on church Websites. Interview people from the pulpit on Sunday morning who can provide glimpses of the vision. Tell stories of other people, churches, and organizations that have accomplished a similar vision. Above all, remember that vision is an inner work. You must believe it to see it. When people buy into you, they buy into your vision.

Take Charge

Last, there are several aspects of leadership, but one of the most basic is simply taking charge. Every organization needs someone who asks the right questions, points the way to the future, and makes certain that necessary tasks are assigned and performed. The quintessential leadership tasks are first choosing the way and then convincing the church constituency that the right way has been selected. This requires communication skills harnessed to an inner vision that captures the future in a way that strikes a chord with the people.

How long does it take for church members to catch the vision? It depends on the size of the vision, but the following chart will help answer that question.

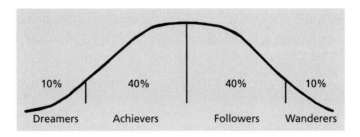

	10%	40%	40%	10%
	Dreamers	Achievers	Followers	Wanderers

When an attempt is made to cast a vision to the people, they naturally align into four groups. The first are the *Dreamers*. Ten percent of the people generally fall into this group, and they grasp the vision very early on, usually within three to six months. Most important, however, is that they see the vision and then help others to see it and do it.

The second group is called *Achievers*. Forty percent of the people will eventually find their way into this grouping. They are the ones who see the vision and do it. It may take as long as eighteen months for some of them to catch the vision, but when they do, they are on the team.

The third group is called *Followers*. They mirror the size of the Achievers with about forty percent of the people. It takes most of them two to three years to catch on to the vision. Unfortunately, even after they see it, they are often content to let others do it.

The last group is called *Wanderers*. They match the Dreamers in size and never seem to buy into the vision. They never see it.

Based on this chart, it takes at least two years to get enough people on board with a vision to move forward. It depends somewhat on the size of the vision. If you are going to distribute videos to all the people in your city, as in my earlier story, you might be able to get people to buy into it sooner. If you are trying to help people see a vision to relocate your church, however, it probably will take much longer. Sometimes what may seem like a simple thing—changing a church's name for instance—will take an extremely long time. I know of one church that took eleven years to change its name! This I know for sure: Having a vision does not guarantee success in reaching it; but you don't have a chance without one.

> We all live under the same sky, but we don't all have the same horizon.

A friend once showed me a card on which was printed his church's vision. It looked somewhat like the following.

Our Vision

To build a loving church family in the midst of broken relationships we will . . .

- relocate to a new campus in five years.
- build a new multipurpose facility.
- have 50 percent of people using their gifts.
- get 80 percent of our people in small groups.
- place a Bible in every home in our city.

Note how the vision is very specific, which is why it is dynamic.

MY PLANNING NOTEBOOK

What we see: Vision

- The greatest leadership gift of all is the gift of vision.

My Comments:

- Nothing becomes dynamic until it becomes specific, and a vision
  statement gives specifics about what our church is going to do and
  where it is heading.

My Comments:

- People commit to vision not mission.

My Comments:

- Vision is an inner work. When people buy into you, they buy into your vision.

My Comments:

- We all live under the same sky, but we don't have the same horizon. What is our church's horizon?

There are so many people who can figure costs,
and so few who can measure values.

—CALIFORNIA TRIBUNE

TWELVE

What We
Believe: Values

One cannot have a real vision for
the future without a sense of
history. The past is a record of the
values that should propel us into
the future. As we move toward the future, it
is important that we look back to discover the values that give meaning
to our ministries, then move forward by building on our values to take
hold of new opportunities. Unfortunately, the strong pull toward the
future often causes us to forget the past.

If looking at our history promotes a Band-Aid mentality of survival—
an effort to hold the church together by looking to the good old days for
affirmation—then looking back is counterproductive. When a church
looks to the past for its sense of pride, it will dwell too much on past
successes. Yet, when a church looks to the past to discover its values,
it can be a powerful link to the future. The past is for remembering,
not reliving. However, looking back is necessary to fund a powerful

future. Martin Marty, a church historian at the University of Chicago, calls this finding a usable future in our past.

Biblical Basis for Values

Is it biblical to look back at our history? In the book of Philippians, the apostle Paul says that he forgets what is behind him and looks forward to the future. Paul says, "forgetting what lies behind and reaching forward to what lies ahead, I press on toward the goal for the prize of the upward call of God in Christ Jesus" (Phil. 3:13–14). Paul is talking about his desire to become like Christ. He means that he does not want to put his confidence in fleshly concerns that once were important to him, like his ethnic heritage and training. In short, he is looking only to his faith in Christ to become more like Christ. He is not speaking about looking back to our history as a local church.

There are other biblical passages, however, that point out the importance of remembering the past. Joshua could have been the first to say, "A good past is the best future."

The story is found in Joshua 4:1–24. After all the people of Israel finished crossing the Jordan River, the Lord spoke to Joshua and commanded that twelve stones be removed from the river and set up as a memorial. After the stones were set up in Gilgal, Joshua explained the reason:

When your children ask their fathers in time to come, saying, "What are these stones?" then you shall inform your children, saying, "Israel crossed this Jordan on dry ground." For the LORD your God dried up the waters of the Jordan before you until you had crossed, just as the LORD your God had done to the Red Sea, which He dried up before us until we had crossed; that all the peoples of the earth may know that the hand of the LORD is mighty, so that you may fear the LORD your God forever. (vv. 21–24)

The Lord knew that it was crucial for Israel to understand the values of the past in order to design a new future. Thus, he commanded that, whenever the nation of Israel struggled with determining direction, the people should always look to the past to rediscover their core values.

Another passage that says it in a different manner is Psalm 22:30–31. One translation paraphrases it, "Our children too shall serve him, for they shall hear from us about the wonders of the Lord; generations yet unborn shall hear of all the miracles he did for us" (TLB).

Looking Back to Find Values

There is a great deal of talk today about defining a church's core values. But it is a mistake to think that we create our values in a vacuum. The truth is we discover them by looking to the past. Just as the people of Israel looked to the past to rebuild their own values, we must look to our church's past to reconstruct ours. We need to create sort of a conversation with the past. I like how Kiyoko Takeda, a professor at International Christian University in Tokyo, Japan says it: "Recognizing what we have done in the past is recognition of ourselves. By conducting a dialogue with our past, we are searching how to go forward."[1] Remember: When you aren't sure where you are going, look to where you've been.

How far back should we look?

It is good to look as far back as possible. It's reported that Winston Churchill once said, "The further backward you can look, the farther forward you can see."[2]

Holding onto our core values is a major concern of people in our churches. With all of the new innovations taking place, people are afraid we may be eroding the values that set the Church apart in the first place. People are fearful about the loss of traditional values in our society. It is one thing to see values eroded on television, but it is quite another to think you see them eroding at church too.

Yet in our desire to hold on to core values, we have to be cautious not to put an unrealistic interpretation on the past. A cartoon I saw a number of years ago featured the apostle Paul. In the cartoon, he had just finished writing the book of Corinthians, and he bemoans the fact that while he addressed problems such as gluttony, party spirit, incest, and other issues, someday people will look back on it all as the "good old days." Ecclesiastes 7:10 says it well: "Do not say, 'Why is it that the former days were better than these?' For it is not from wisdom that you ask about this." The good old days were never as good as we think they were. In fact, I have been told that the only reason we think the past was so good is that as we grow older, the number of things that annoy us increases.

When we were children, we did not pay much attention to bad things. We focused on playing and did not think much about the news of wars in other countries, murders taking place in our own cities, or people deceiving others. Only when we became adults did we begin to notice such happenings. The world has always had its share of problems, we just were not aware of them when we were young. Thus, we tend to think of the past, during our younger days, as being the good ones. The truth is they were never quite as good as we remember them. There is no better way to waste time in life than to dwell on the past. We should learn from the past with as much objectivity as possible, and then move on.

Where Values Fit

So, how do past values fit in? Values are an anchor in the constant sea of change. The methods by which we do ministry change over time, but the values remain the ties to the past and the future. Going back to the illustration of a hot air balloon, it would look like the following.

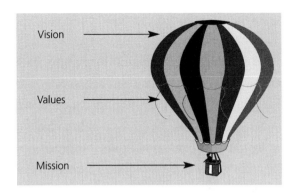

The mission is the biblical reason we exist as a church, illustrated in my sketch by the basket in which people ride. If you have ever seen a hot air balloon, you have probably noticed that the baskets on all the balloons look pretty much the same. In the same way, the mission statements of various churches are pretty much the same. They may be stated quite differently, but a close look will demonstrate they are much the same. For instance, I used to attend a church that said its mission was to "Know Christ and Make Him Known." A few years later, I attended a church that said its mission was to "Win People to Christ and Build Them Up in the Faith." These two churches stated their mission differently, but essentially they were the same.

The vision is illustrated in this sketch by the balloon. The vision of churches will vary greatly, sort of like the colors and designs of hot air balloons. However, the seams that bind the balloon together are the values. The values of a church are what hold the vision together. As we seek to move forward using new methods and ministries, the values keep us tied to our roots. Obviously, if a hot air balloon developed a tear in one of its seams, it would spell disaster. Even a small tear in a seam, producing a slow leak, would result in a problem fairly quickly. This is the situation in which many churches find themselves. They may have developed a mission statement and a vision statement, but they did not tie them all together with their values.

So, what are values, and how do we find them? Core values are what a church stands for or holds dear. They are the heart and soul of the church. They are the beliefs upon which a church bases its decisions; or perhaps another way to say it is: They are what's really important. The problem is that values are usually unwritten and unrecognized. They're called *tacit* values, that is, unwritten values. When a church first starts to define its values, it usually has a difficult time figuring out what they are. While they know values exist and have a major role in decision-making, they cannot seem to find a way to state them.

A creative tool that helps people identify a church's core values is using the church name as an acrostic. People are able to verbalize ingrained values of their church by listing them as an acrostic of their name. Notice the values of Grace Church in this illustration.

Grace Church

Our Mission: To prepare people to be followers of Jesus Christ.

Our Values:
- Genuine Christian Living
- Reaching the Lost
- Authentic Worship
- Continuous Growth
- Excellence in Ministry

The church is committed to the authority of Scripture and believes the Bible reveals the person of God and how people should live their Christian lives. Its aim is to present the claims of Jesus Christ in ways that will effectively reach our postmodern society. Thus, its core values are listed under five major headings.

The first core value is *genuine Christian living*. That means the people of Grace Church will seek to disciple their own people into deeper relationships of honesty, love, and service.

The second value is *reaching the lost*. They believe it is crucial to use as many means as possible to reach people for Christ because lost people matter to God.

The third value is *authentic worship*. Grace Church believes God is worthy of worship, and desires to give him praise.

Their fourth value is *continuous growth*. To them, growth has a two-fold dimension: quality and quantity. They are called to assist people in developing a biblical worldview that affects their beliefs, values, and behaviors, but they also feel it is important to find and fold the lost into their church body.

The fifth and last core value is *excellence in ministry*. The people of Grace Church believe they must do the best they can with what God has given them.

Discovering Your Church's Values

Using an acrostic is a key, creative tool to surface core values. But the following are specific steps you can use to arrive at the final version of your church's core values.

The first thing to do is to ask people to give you a list of the values they think you should hold on to no matter what. Start with the senior pastor; then take his or her list to the staff and main board and ask them to add to it. Compile the answers into a revised version and hand it out to all ministry leaders, asking them to add to it. Once you receive all of their replies, take the entire list and revise it again.

Keep careful track of the statements or phrases that are mentioned numerous times. On occasion you will have to do some interpreting. For instance, some people may list Sunday school, Sunday evening worship, and vacation Bible school as values. These are ministry programs rather than values, but try to find the hidden value beneath the program. In your conversations, you may determine that in the minds of our people, Sunday school expressed the value of education, so you could state it as continuous growth. The value beneath Sunday evening worship might be fellowship, which you could state as genuine Christian living. The underlying value of VBS is outreach, which we stated as reaching the lost. As you work through this process, your core values will emerge.

Sometimes using a survey tool is helpful in discovering a church's core values. The following is a survey tool that churches have found useful. Feel free to duplicate it for use in your own church. Survey a minimum of 15 percent of your people and add up the points for each of the ten categories to see what your people honestly value.

Defining Core Values

You have ten points to divide up among the following values. Some may receive no points, while others may receive many. Think about your church and then divide the ten points according to your perception of what is important in your church.

Authentic Community _____
- Community groups
- Honest relationships
- Transparent and vulnerable

Team Ministry _____
- Valuing each other
- Protecting each other
- Serving in area of strength

Active Prayer _____
- Individual
- Corporate
- Modeled by leaders

Creative Atmosphere _____
- Flexible programming
- Sacrificial attitude
- Comfortable feeling

Empowered Believers _____
- Pastors as equippers
- Gift-based service
- Passion-based service

Blended Worship _____
- Value all styles
- Use all styles
- Involve all generations

Biblical Focus _____
- Preaching
- Teaching
- Practice

Transformational Growth _____
- Call to commitment
- Challenging believers
- Life change

Effective Evangelism _____
- Local or international
- Church planting
- Community service

Servant Leadership _____
- Humble
- Sacrificial
- Models

Look Back, Leap Forward

The principle to keep in mind is to look back to find your values, but look forward to find your methods. When you first begin talking about stating core values, a large number of your people may assume it means reviving former programs or ministries. However, that is not what is intended at all. For example, a few years ago, Grace Church had to cancel its Sunday evening worship service. At the time the service was cancelled, over two hundred adults were attending on Sunday morning, but only about twenty adults on Sunday evenings. The decision was made that they could not continue the evening service. Later, when church leaders began the process of planning, many assumed the church would revive the old Sunday evening worship service. The purpose of planning, however, was to discover the values underneath the old programming, not to revive the old programming. Fortunately, church leaders understood the principle that you look back to find your values; you leap forward to find your methods.

What the leaders did was to develop a new small group ministry on Sunday evenings, built on the core values of the past. Church leaders determined that the core value underneath the evening worship service was fellowship, or genuine Christian living. In addition, other values represented in the evening worship service were authentic worship and continuous growth. Rather than simply trying to revive the old method of Sunday evening worship, the leaders looked forward for a new method that would fulfill the same values, but be culturally relevant today.

What they finally chose to do was to begin a small group ministry on Sunday evenings in the homes of various members. Small group ministry carries on the core values of the former Sunday evening worship service, but presents them in a way that is relevant to today's church members. For example, small groups allow for fellowship or genuine Christian living, authentic worship, and continuous growth. And you know what happened? Grace Church went from only twenty people attending Sunday evening worship to over one hundred people participating in small groups on the same evening. They looked back to identify the core values underneath Sunday evening worship, but then leapt forward to find a ministry method that would carry on those core values.

Here is another example of what one church is doing right now that is based on the same process. One church leader tells her story this way.

I've worked in vacation Bible school (VBS) for nearly twenty-five years. Why, I can remember when we had more children attend our two-week VBS than attended on an average Sunday morning. However, a few years ago we noticed that fewer and fewer children were taking advantage of this ministry. So, we began the look back, leap forward process. First, we looked back to identify the core values beneath VBS. After talking with people who had been involved with this program for many years, we determined the core value of VBS for our church was evangelism. We then leapt forward to see if there was a new way we could evangelize children that would be more effective today. We discovered that youth soccer has become a major enterprise in our community. One of our fathers brought us some research that confirmed more children are participating in youth soccer in our city than in any other activity. After doing some basic research, we also found out that several of our members are already coaching youth soccer. The short story is we are not going to do a traditional VBS this coming summer. Instead, we are going to offer a weeklong soccer camp from 9:00 a.m. to 1:00 p.m., Monday through Saturday. The camp will focus on teaching children soccer skills, but during their break times and at lunch, one of the coaches will be telling a Bible story, and one will be sharing his or her testimony with the children and how to become a Christian. An invitation will be given each day for children to accept Christ as their personal Savior. On Saturday, parents of the children will be invited to attend a demonstration of what their kids have learned. They'll play a short soccer game and end with a barbecue lunch. All parents will be given a packet of information on soccer skills, but the packet will also include information on how to become a believer in Christ, as well as information on our church's ministry.[3]

Can you see what this church is doing? They are carrying on the core values of VBS but using a new method, or ministry, that is relevant to children and parents today.

The key principle to keep in mind as you discover your core values is to look back to find your values, but to look forward to find your methods. Never get values and methods confused. Values are the unwritten foundation for the various ministries or church practices, but they are not the ministries themselves.

MY PLANNING NOTEBOOK

What we believe: Values

- The past is for remembering not reliving.

My Comments:

- Values are the unseen beliefs that we hold as important.

My Comments:

- Using an acrostic of our church name is a simple way to list our core values.

My Comments:

- Look back to discover our core values, but look forward to determine our ministries.

NOTES

1. Kiyoko Takeda, quoted by Henry O. Dormann in *The Speaker's Book of Quotations* (New York: Fawcett Columbine, 1987), 92.

2. Quoted by Os Guinness in *Steering Through Chaos* (Colorado Springs: NavPress, 2000), 9.

3. Confidential letter in author files.

Goals help to crystallize your thinking. Develop plans and deadlines; develop sincere desire to achieve; develop confidence and determination.

—FLOYD KEITH

THIRTEEN

What We Achieve: Goals

Have you heard of the Nine Pregnant Women rule? It takes nine months to have a baby, but you cannot have a baby in one month with nine pregnant women. It takes time for the natural process to develop! This rule applies to any project. After writing your mission, vision, and values, it is time to identify which steps you must complete sequentially over the necessary period of time it will take to accomplish your vision.

These steps are called *goals*. Goals must be completed to reach the vision, and it is best to think big but start small. It is necessary to think big about your vision, but it is equally important to start small by setting some reachable and controllable goals.

Adding the dimension of goals to the balloon illustration, our plan begins to look like the following.

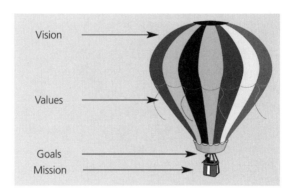

Vision

Values

Goals
Mission

Goals serve as steps to move from the mission to the accomplishment of the vision. The goals are like tether lines that tie the mission, vision, and values together. As each of the goals is achieved, you get close to the accomplishment of the mission and the vision.

Developing Mission Goals

When churches develop goals, they typically review what was accomplished or not accomplished in the last year. Then they set goals for the next year based on what is left over from the last year and add a few new goals. There is a better way to do it.

There are two types of goals: survival goals and mission goals. When a church focuses on what has not happened in the past, it is developing survival goals. When a church focuses on what can happen in the future, it is developing mission goals. The following chart depicts some of the differences between these two types of goals.

To begin developing mission goals, look at the mission itself and dream big about what God wants your church to do in the future. Rather than building on what was not accomplished last year, a church should basically begin with a fresh slate each year and think about what God wants to do in the coming year. Financial planners call this zero-based budgeting, that is you zero out last year's budget and begin from scratch to build a new budget for the coming year. I guess you could call ours a zero-based goal setting process. Zero out last year's goals and set new goals for the next year.

Survival Goals	Mission Goals
1. Focus on what has not happened	1. Focus on what can happen
2. Produce remedial solutions	2. Produce innovative solutions
3. Based on the past	3. Based on the future
4. Doubt based	4. Dream based
5. Identify problems	5. Identify potential
6. Lower congregational morale	6. Raise congregational morale
7. Demand low level of faith	7. Demand high level of faith

Here is how to go about developing mission goals.

Organize Goal-Setting Teams

First, organize a team of three people representing each area of church ministry. For example: worship, adult education, facilities, and so forth. Second, provide each team with a copy of your mission, vision, and values. Then ask each team to meet with other people from their area of ministry and develop as many goals as they can think of that God might want them to accomplish in the coming five to ten years. Expect them to set basic goals, like reviewing curriculum, as well as long-term goals, like hiring a new staff member. Ask them to dream big and not to limit their thinking of what God might want for their area of ministry. Someone once remarked that when it comes to goals we should shoot for the moon. Even if you miss, you will end up among the stars.

Each team must come up with a minimum of nine goals, but if they have more, that is great. All of their goals must contribute in some way to accomplish the overall mission and vision, as well as remaining true to the core values. If you think you might end up with way too many goals, you are right. So help your leaders narrow their goals to what must be accomplished in the short-range, mid-range, and long-range. But this is getting a bit ahead of the process. Let us back up a step or two.

Conduct a Planning Meeting

After the various teams put together their lists of goals, then schedule an open space planning meeting. This is a way to create excitement and inspiration among everyone to accomplish the mission and vision of a church. Find a room large enough for everyone to attend, and remove all of the furniture except folding chairs. A fellowship hall, gym, or other similar room works very well. Arrange the chairs in a circle so people can see each other. After all the participants arrive, give a short opening statement about your mission, vision, and core values, reminding everyone in attendance that whatever goals they arrive at must fit these key guidelines for your church ministry.

Distribute large sheets of paper and markers to each team, and then dismiss the teams to different locations in the room. After each team regroups, their job is to take all of the goals they have, plus any new ones they may think of, and prioritize them into short-range, medium-range, and long-range goals. Any goal that can be accomplished in less than two years is considered short-range. Goals that will take between three and five years to complete are medium-range. Anything that takes longer than five years is a long-range goal.

Let the teams debate the order of priority for all their goals and write them on the blank sheets of paper. As each team completes it's prioritized list, tape their sheets of paper on one of the walls in the room. This is typically a good time to break for refreshment and fellowship.

After the break, the entire group comes together and someone from each ministry team reads and explains his or her team's goals to the larger group. All of the participants are encouraged to ask questions and make suggestions for all areas of ministry. This open space meeting encourages everyone to look at all goals with fresh eyes and to offer suggestions. Some of your break-through ideas come from people outside of a particular ministry.

The entire open space planning meeting usually takes from three to five hours. Once all teams have had an opportunity to share their goals and answer questions, the meeting is over. However, sometimes break-out groups will continue to develop their goals. For instance, if one of the ministry teams is wrestling with determining its goals, they may continue to meet as a breakout group. When this happens, anyone from the larger group who wishes to stay and help is welcome to do so. Later on, each team turns in its list of goals to the chairperson of the planning team. The chairperson puts all of the goals together into a rough draft long-range plan.

Here is a sample of what the worship team from one church listed as their short-range, medium-range, and long-range goals.

Worship Goals

Short-Range (1–2 years)	Target Date
• Train prayer counselors for worship prayer time.	May 4
• Purchase a video projector.	June 1
• Fine-tune guest registration procedure.	September 15

Medium-Range (3–5 years)
• Recruit a drama team and begin a drama ministry.
• Place sound baffles in the worship center to dampen noise.
• Install new carpet in the worship center to update style and color.

Long-Range (6–10 years)
• Develop and use videos in worship service.
• Hire a worship arts pastor.
• Purchase a new sound system.

Evaluate Each Team's Goals

The planning team should meet to go over the rough draft of goals. Here, evaluate all of the goals against the following three questions:

- Do the goals sustain the mission of our church?
- Do the goals move us toward our vision?
- Do the goals uphold our core values?

Each ministry's goals will be designed specifically for that ministry. However, all of the goals must help move the church toward its larger mission and vision. Additional goals are added from the P Team and the F Team to round out the entire plan.

All short-range goals must include timelines. A wise pastor once commented that goals are dreams with deadlines. As illustrated in the worship goals above, target dates have been set for all the goals in the short-range category.

Churches are learning that things are changing so fast in today's world it does not help to set dates beyond one or two years. Since goals are set each year, the ones in the medium-range and long-range categories are often moved up to short-range during the next planning session. Or, they are dropped entirely. Sometimes leaders set medium-range and long-range goals only to discover that God leads in a different direction later on. Try to remain flexible to the leading of the Holy Spirit, while at the same time maintaining a sense of direction. The Bible verse that directs us in this process is Proverbs 16:9, "The mind of man plans his way, But the Lord directs his steps." God wants us to plan a direction, but to be flexible enough to change directions as he leads us.

Yogi Berra once said, "If you don't know where you're going, you'll end up someplace else." Without clear goals, you will end up somewhere; it just may not be where you desired to be.

MY PLANNING NOTEBOOK

What we achieve: Goals

- When it comes to goals, think big but start small.

My Comments:

- We need to shoot for the moon. Even if we miss it, we will end up among the stars.

My Comments:

- Goals are dreams with deadlines.

My Comments:

- Each of our church's ministries needs to write nine goals: three short-range, three mid-range, and three long-range.

My Comments:

Planning is bringing the future into the present
so you can do something about it now.

—ALAN LAKEIN

FOURTEEN

The Planning Gap

O vercoming obstacles is just part of life. Sometimes the obstacles are real, while other times they are just our perceptions. A few years ago, I was driving an unfamiliar road, almost late for an appointment. Ahead of me, I saw a train apparently blocking the road. Fearing that a delay would make me late, I began to look for alternate roads, but finding none, I continued toward the train. As I got closer, I realized, the train was on an overpass, and the road that seemed to be blocked went under the train. Had I tried other roads, I would have surely been late. I learned an important lesson that day: Many times obstacles in the distance seem impassable, but when we persevere, they disappear. At other times the obstacles are real. One aspect of leadership is learning how to see the real obstacles early on and to devise a plan to overcome them.

> Do not be afraid of setting goals simply because some past goals were not reached. Remember: If you push the limits today, you do what was impossible yesterday.

One of the reasons people are reluctant to take part in a church's long-range planning team is a lingering frustration they have from serving on ineffective committees. Many of the plans and goals developed in past committees were never completed. People are just too busy to spend time serving on a long-range planning team that does not produce something worthwhile. People have less than three hours to devote to ministry outside of Sunday morning worship. Hence, people in our church are very selective regarding service in ministry or on a committee. That is why it is so important to have a clear statement of mission, vision, and values. People must sense their service is of real value to the overall direction of the church's ministry.

A planning gap exists when the plans and goals are not implemented. This occurs when a plan is developed without properly aligning the resources that are needed to actually see the plans fulfilled. For example, if a church develops a plan to use projection of songs in its worship service, it must align enough financial resources so a projector, screen, and other necessary components may be purchased. Failure to budget enough money for the project leads to a planning gap (see figure below).

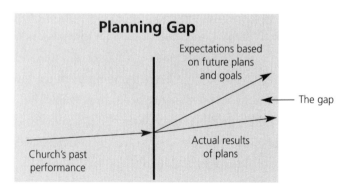

Planning Gap

Expectations based on future plans and goals

The gap

Actual results of plans

Church's past performance

Four M's of Alignment

The answer is to employ the four principles of alignment. I call them the Four M's of Alignment, and they are the ingredients for overcoming barriers to your goals. Highly successful leaders employ these Four M's with great consistency. They are manpower, money, management, and ministry of prayer.

What is alignment? Alignment is the intentional organizing of a church's practices and behaviors so that they are consistent with its stated mission, vision, values, and goals.

The biggest hurdle to seeing your church's goals fulfilled is internal misalignment. A church can set wonderful goals, but if the church's organization does not align in support of the goals, most will fail. The main obstacle to overcome in reaching your goals is internal rather than external.

Manpower

The first principle of alignment is manpower. The manpower of the church must be deployed to fulfill its mission, vision, values, and goals. This is clearly an internal issue. One of the main obstacles to overcome in reaching goals is the lack of people support. For a goal to be accomplished, it must have sufficient people devoting their talents and energies to seeing it fulfilled. When you set a goal, you need to ask yourself, "How can I make sure people are working toward the achievement of this goal?" If you cannot align people with the goal, there is a high probability it will not be reached.

Money

Money is the second key to alignment. We do not like to talk about money too much in churches, but the reality is we cannot do much without it. Not only the manpower, but also the money of the church must be deployed to fulfill its mission, vision, values, and goals. This is where the budget of the church comes into play. A church must ask the question, "Is the budget supporting the accomplishment of the church's goals?" Someone once remarked that we can tell our priorities by looking at our checkbooks. The same can be said for our church. What does our church's checkbook say about its commitment to its mission, vision, values, and goals? When it comes to money, we must remember the cost of doing nothing is greater than the cost of doing something.

One of the major obstacles to overcome in reaching goals is the lack of financial support. A few years ago, a church I consulted became concerned that it was not effectively reaching new people for Christ. Someone suggested they evaluate how much money was spent on outreach to their local community. After a bit of research, they were shocked to discover that in their entire budget of 189,000 dollars only 500 dollars was going toward outreach. Money was not aligned with their evangelistic goal. When you develop your plans, be sure to think about how you will align the church's finances to support your goals.

Management

Management is the third key ingredient to successful goal completion. The management of the church's calendar should be deployed to fulfill its mission, vision, values, and goals. As I discussed earlier, people have only so much time to devote to ministry today. Thus, wise church leaders will carefully plan the church's calendar so that it directs people toward fulfillment of its goals rather than away from them. Church leaders should ask the question, "Does our calendar of events reflect our mission, vision, values, and goals?"

Think of it this way. If the average person only gives three hours to church activities beyond the Sunday worship service, then we need to be certain the opportunities offered point us in the direction of our mission, vision, values, and goals. I think this is why so many people today do not attend everything the church offers. Years ago it was common practice for people to go to church every time the doors were open. But there is so much more competition for our time today that people must make choices. People are astute enough to see that some events the church offers are not as strategic as others. One of the reasons churches are streamlining their programming is related to this principle of alignment. Time is so valuable today that an effective church must carefully align its programming so that it supports its goals.

Worship Goals

Short-Range (1–2 years)	Target Date
• Train prayer counselors for worship prayer time.	May 4
• Purchase a video projector.	June 1
• Fine-tune guest registration procedure.	September 15

Medium-Range (3–5 years)
• Recruit a drama team and begin a drama ministry.
• Place sound baffles in the worship center to dampen noise.
• Install new carpet in the worship center to update style and color.

Long-Range (6–10 years)
• Develop and use videos in worship service.
• Hire a worship arts pastor.
• Purchase a new sound system.

Alignment

Manpower:	Bill S. will train prayer counselors.
	Bob R. will purchase a video projector.
	Mary W. will develop a new registration procedure.
Money:	$100 is budgeted for training prayer counselors.
	$2,500 is budgeted for a video projector.
	$500 is budgeted for a new registration process.
Management:	Prayer counselors will serve in only one service a month.
	Bob R. has full authority to purchase a projector.
	Mary W. is relieved of other responsibilities.
Ministry of Prayer:	Prayer counselors will hold a quarterly prayer retreat.
	Joe and Sylvia J. will pray for Bob's purchase of projector.
	Mary W. to recruit a prayer team for new guests.

Ministry of Prayer

The last key to alignment is the ministry of prayer. A church's ministry of prayer should be deployed to fulfill its mission, vision, values, and goals. Now, all churches pray, but most do not strategically pray in a way that aligns their prayer ministry with the goals of the church. For example, how many churches have prayer intercessors specifically aligned to pray for worship, facilities, or youth? One of the reasons some churches do so well in reaching goals is that they actually recruit people to pray specifically in line with their mission, vision, values, and goals. Refer to the plan on the previous page to see how alignment is applied to a church's worship goals.

As you can see, each of the Four M's are aligned with short-range goals. By doing this, this church addresses the major obstacles ahead of time.

A pastor friend likes to tell a story about African gazelles. According to him, the African gazelle can leap thirty feet horizontally and ten feet vertically. Yet, can be easily kept in any enclosure with a wooden or solid fence only three feet high. Gazelles will not jump over anything, unless they can easily see exactly where their feet will land. Like a gazelle, our goals can sometimes be stopped by the simplest of things. The question is, "What are the three-foot fences that hold us in?" In most situations, our controlling fences or obstacles can be addressed by answering these questions:

- The Manpower Question: Is the manpower of our church deployed to fulfill our goals?
- The Money Question: Is the money of our church deployed to fulfill our goals?
- The Management Question: Is the schedule of our church deployed to fulfill our goals?
- The Ministry of Prayer Question: Is the prayer of our church deployed to fulfill our goals?

It may be helpful to think of these Four M's in different terms. For example, you might prefer asking if your goals are aligned with the congregation (manpower), checkbook (money), calendar (management), and contemplation (prayer). Or, you could use the words *talent*, *treasure*, *time*, and *trajectory*.

You may have never considered the necessity of aligning these aspects of ministry to advance your goals. Most people have not and that is one reason goals do not get accomplished. But, as a friend of mine told me once, do not let yourself feel discouraged just because there is a fence on this side of the pasture; the gate may be open on the other side.

There are two other obstacles that we often face when setting goals of which you should be aware. First, goals need to address situations we can control. Let me give you an example. The first time I served on a planning team, I was on the evangelism council. We set a goal to win one hundred people to Christ in twelve months. Now that is a fine goal, but the truth is we cannot control what other people do. The goal is not controllable, and it set us up for failure right from the beginning. I discovered it was better to write the goal in a manner that we could control. In my research, I found that 12 percent of the people who visited our church ended up receiving Christ as their Savior. Using that percentage as our guideline, we determined that we needed to attract twelve hundred new people to church in twelve months in order to see one hundred people come to Christ. So, we set a goal of inviting twelve hundred guests to attend our church in twelve months, or one hundred guests per month. We could control that goal by developing ways to attract that many guests to church.

Thus we restated the goal in a way that we could do some planning from our end toward its accomplishment. God wants both our prayer and our participation. He tells us in 1 Corinthians 3:6, "I planted the seed, Apollos watered it, but God made it grow" (NIV). It could be stated this way: Without God, we cannot do anything; without us, God may not do anything. God certainly does not need us, but he chooses to work through us.

Second, your goals need to be reachable. That church sincerely believed it could reach one hundred new people for Christ in one year's time. If, on the other hand, we had said one thousand people, it would not have been realistic. It is important to keep in mind that a goal needs to be large enough to stretch the faith of your people without discouraging them.

MY PLANNING NOTEBOOK

The planning gap:

- A planning gap exists when goals are not implemented.

My Comments:

- The way to overcome the planning gap is to align our goals with the Four M's of manpower, money, management, and ministry of prayer.

*It may be alright to be content with what you have;
never with what you are.*

—B. C. FORBES

FIFTEEN

Build Your Dream House

The end product of the planning process is a written plan for the future of your church's ministry. The plan is based on the mission, vision, and values of your church. Its development takes into serious consideration both the past history of your church, and its future opportunities and it's current situation and future realities.

In some ways, the process is more important than the end product. One of the key elements in helping a church develop one mind and heart for the future is to help the people go through the process together.

A successful plan will be the acrostic POLS. The *P* equals the purpose of the church. Under purpose is your mission, vision, and values. The purpose must come first for effective ministry. The *O* equals organization. Under organization are the two M's: money and ministry of prayer. Next is *L*, which stands for leadership. Of course, this relates to the manpower. Lastly is the *S*, which stands for supervision or in the terms of alignment—management. Develop your long-range plan in the exact order of POLS. Some churches have tried doing it backward, but it does not work. It actually turns out so awful that some say, if you do it backwards you'll get SLOP.

Putting It All Together

View your church as a building. The top part is for *dreaming*. It is at this level that the mission, vision, and values of a church are developed. The second level is for *designing*. At this second level the short-range, medium-range, and long-range goals are developed. The lower level is for *doing*. At this level, the actual work of ministry is done.

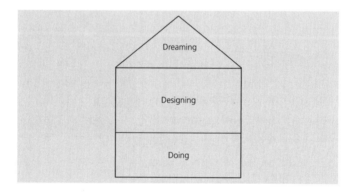

As you can see, the dreaming level covers the entire structure. You might think of it as the roof of a house. The roof covers the house providing protection and a unity of structure. Thus, the mission, vision, and values of a church provide a covering for all of a church's ministries.

Dreaming is mainly the responsibility of the senior pastor and the major board of a church. For most churches, it is best if they revisit their dream about every three to five years.

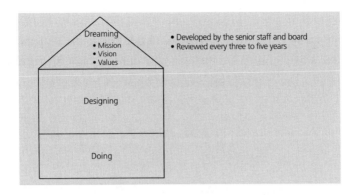

The designing level is where the ministries of a church are to be found. In larger churches, staff members usually lead the various ministries. In smaller churches, there is a committee, or perhaps board members, assigned to each area of ministry. All of the ministries fit under the roof of the building, that is, they build toward the mission, vision, and values of the total church. The ministries listed are just a sample of what many churches do. The idea is that each ministry must contribute in some manner to the mission, vision, and values of the total church. It is at this level that the goals are developed for each area of ministry. In addition, the P Teams and F Teams function at this level. Goals are developed at this level each year.

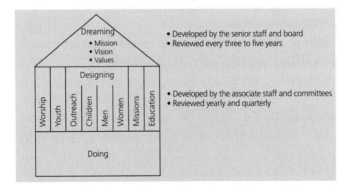

The bottom floor is where the day-to-day, week-to-week, and month-to-month ministry takes place. That is why it is called the doing level. Most of a church's volunteers and support staff are located on this level. Plans at this level are developed and reviewed quarterly, monthly, and weekly.

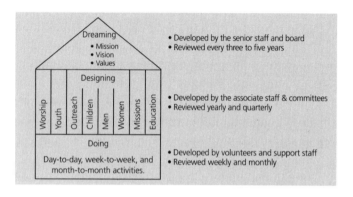

It is clear that the planning process begins at the top and works its way toward the bottom. First, a church looks back to identify its mission and values. Second, it develops a vision for the future based on those criteria. Third, a church looks back to identify its core values. Fourth, a church establishes goals that will take it step by step toward its mission, vision, and values. Last, a church aligns the Four M's so that the day-do-day work of the church supports the overall mission, vision, values, and goals.

As an example, here is a complete copy of the current plan for the worship ministry that Grace Church developed.

Charting the Future: A Worship Ministry Plan for Grace Church

Our Mission (What We Do)

The mission of Grace Church is to prepare people to be followers of Jesus Christ.

Our Mission Expanded (How We Will Do Ministry)

Grace Church exists to *present* Christ to people in a:

- Creative—using new, innovative methods
- Compelling—in the power of the Holy Spirit
- Caring—within sensitive, compassionate relationships

way and to *prepare* them to be followers of Jesus Christ who are:

- Committed to the Word—growing in maturity
- Committed to Serve—giving in time, talent, and treasure
- Committed to Others—caring for one another.

Our Vision (What We See)

We the people of Grace Church have a vision to build a strong and loving church in the midst of broken relationships. To accomplish this vision we will:

- Relocate to a new campus within five years.
- Build a new multipurpose facility with ten years.
- Involve 50 percent of our people in the use of their spiritual gifts.
- Get 80 percent of our adult worshipers in small groups.
- Place a Bible in every home in our city within five years.

Our Values (What We Believe)

The values that tend to drive our ministry are:

Genuine Christian Living
Reaching the Lost
Authentic Worship
Continuous Growth
Excellence in Ministry

Each area of ministry has its own specific plan, and they are formulated in the same manner as the worship plan (see Appendix B).

You may be surprised at all the hard work that goes into formulating such a plan, but it takes a lot of unspectacular preparation to produce spectacular results. So prepare your church for opportunities, and then let those opportunities find you! And, when you have completed your entire comprehensive plan, look back with satisfaction, but forward in anticipation of what God is going to do in and through your church.

Our Worship Goals (What We Will Achieve)

Short-Range (1–2 years)	Target Date
• Train prayer counselors for worship prayer time.	May 4
• Purchase a video projector.	June 1
• Fine-tune guest registration procedure.	September 15

Medium-Range (3–5 years)
- Recruit a drama team and begin a drama ministry.
- Place sound baffles in the worship center to dampen noise.
- Install new carpet in the worship center to update style and color.

Long-Range (6–10 years)
- Develop and use videos in worship service.
- Hire a worship arts pastor.
- Purchase a new sound system.

Alignment

Manpower:	Bill S. will train prayer counselors.
	Bob R. will purchase a video projector.
	Mary W. will develop a new registration procedure.
Money:	$100 is budgeted for training prayer counselors.
	$2,500 is budgeted for a video projector.
	$500 is budgeted for a new registration process.
Management:	Prayer counselors will serve in only one service a month.
	Bob R. has full authority to purchase a projector.
	Mary W. is relieved of other responsibilities.
Ministry of Prayer:	Prayer counselors will hold a quarterly prayer retreat.
	Joe and Sylvia J. will pray for Bob's purchase of projector.
	Mary W. to recruit a prayer team for new guests.

MY PLANNING NOTEBOOK

Putting it all together:

- Our church is like a house with three floors: dreaming, designing, and doing.

My Comments:

- The designing and doing floors must contribute to the fulfillment of the dream floor.

My Comments:

- We need to prepare ourselves for opportunities, then let those opportunities find us.

My Comments:

- When we finish our plan, we should look back with satisfaction and forward in anticipation.

My Comments:

Appendix A
Worksheets

SWOT Analysis of Our Church

1. What are the *strengths* of our church?

2. What are the *weaknesses* of our church?

3. What are the ministry *opportunities* that exist for our church?

4. What are the *threats* or obstacles that hinder us from taking advantage of the opportunities?

5. If we were starting our church today, what would we . . .
   - Preserve?

   - Modify?

   - Delete?

   - Add?

Ministry Plan Goals

Short-Range (0–2 years)

1.

2.

3.

Medium-Range (3–5 years)

4.

5.

6.

Long-Range (5–10 years)

7.

8.

9.

Ministry Plan Alignment				
Goal and Target Date	Manpower	Money	Management	Ministry of Prayer
1.				
2.				
3.				
4.				
5.				
6.				
7.				
8.				
9.				
10.				

Appendix B

Sample Plan

Purpose

The purpose of _____ (church name) is to glorify God by finding, keeping, and building people.

Our Vision

We, the people of _____ (church name), have a vision to reach the people of _____ (city) for Christ through aggressive proclamation of the gospel to support our group ministries, our preschool, and the lifestyles of our people.

We have a vision to build leadership by training 10 percent of our members to lead small groups. It is our intent to care for our people by involving a minimum of 50 percent of our participants in small groups where they can know and support one another.

We have a vision to encourage 10 percent of our leaders to branch off and plant a new local church approximately every three years.

Our Values

_____ (church name) is strongly committed to the Word of God as our only standard for truth and practice. We stress practical preaching and teaching, which will lead our people into a biblical walk in their daily living.

We are committed to discipling each other through personal relationships both formal and informal. We emphasize accountability through friendships, small groups, and various ministry teams. We maintain friendly, open relationships to all but place a special emphasis on families.

We are Christ's body and serve each other through the use of our spiritual gifts. We desire to be the presence of God in our community and a place where people may come for healing, growing, and serving. In addition, the values which tend to drive our ministry are:

Commitment to each other

Obedience to God

Ministry to people who are hurting

Missions both at home and around the world

Unity in our diversity

New styles of ministry

Involvement with the unchurched

Training for service

Yielding to the Spirit

Our Proposed Goals

Worship

Short-Range (1–2 years)   *Target Date*

Train counselors for prayer and counseling   September 9
   of people during worship.

Develop way to give announcements on slides.   October 1

Fine-tune visitor and member registration   August 15
   procedure.

Medium-Range (3–5 years)

Develop a drama ministry.

Get better noise control.

Increase awareness of need for financial stewardship.

Long-Range (6–10 years)

Hold celebration rehearsals with all participants.

Develop and use visuals (DVDs and slides) more in worship.

Remodel auditorium to keep colors and styles up-to-date.

Music

Short-Range (1–2 years)	*Target Date*
Convert overheads to slides and purchase new projector with brighter light.	January 4
Purchase keyboard for adult worship.	February 1
Purchase and install motorized screen in worship center.	June 4

Medium-Range (3–5 years)

Expand worship teams.

Expand instrumentation.

Purchase three additional cordless microphones.

Long-Range (6–10 years)

Hire a full-time worship leader.

Move sound room and improve lighting.

Host four quarterly concerts for the entire city.

Outreach

Short-Range (1–2 years)	*Target Date*
Recruit an advertising team.	September 15
Develop an advertising plan for _____ (church name).	December 1
Print and distribute church business cards to all members.	January 4

Medium-Range (3–5 years)

Purchase and install a new sign for increased visibility.

Continue and improve homeless outreach.

Continue and improve Right to Life ministry.

Long-Range (6–10 years)

Train 50 percent of all members in lifestyle evangelism.

Develop a school sports outreach in cooperation with youth ministry.

Host city-wide prayer concerts.

Assimilation

Short-Range (1–2 years)	*Target Date*
Design a new church brochure for distribution to visitors.	October 15
Recruit, train, and deploy parking attendants.	August 28
Improve nursery care for members and visitors.	February 1

Medium-Range (3–5 years)

Redecorate physical plant.

Research and develop strategies for increasing second service attendance.

Appoint an assimilation task force to review our assimilation process.

Long-Range (6–10 years)

Organize a tele-care ministry.

Design and print a map of the _____ (church name) facility.

Track membership attendance as a means of stopping drop-outs.

Missions

Short-Range (1–2 years)	*Target Date*
Complete adopt-a-people project.	March 3
Complete two-way accountability with missionaries.	November 15
Continue to expand short-term missions program.	January 4

Medium-Range (3–5 years)

Increase revenue to missions.

Develop a missions room in the church facility.

Design a strategy for communicating missions to the total congregation.

Long-Range (6–10 years)

Hire a staff person for missions

Involve 10 percent of our people in cross-cultural missions.

Plant a church in an unreached people group.

Youth Ministry

Short-Range (1–2 years)	*Target Date*
Expand facilities to increase room for youth ministry.	October 31
Continue to finance existing intern and add a second intern.	January 4
Train staff for youth ministry.	March 4

Medium-Range (3–5 years)

Organize sports or alternative outreach events.

Continue to develop worship team and band.

Develop a standardized doctrinal curriculum.

Long-Range (6–10 years)

Begin a campus ministry.

Purchase a van.

Hire a secretary for youth pastor.

Children's Ministry

Short-Range (1–2 years)	*Target Date*
Expand facility, especially nursery and office space.	April 15
Develop a plan to involve more people in children's ministry.	September 1
Develop a mid-week program for children.	August 15

Medium-Range (3–5 years)

　　Purchase a computer and copy machine for children's ministry.

　　Develop a strategy to advertise children's ministry.

　　Plan a family outreach event.

Long-Range (6–10 years)

　　Hire a full-time assistant children's director.

　　Develop more outside play area for children.

　　Begin a preschool or after school program.

Adult Ministry

Short-Range (1–2 years)	*Target Date*
Hire a part-time intern.	September 1
Begin additional enrichment classes.	September 15
Remodel existing facility into a multipurpose room.	January 15

Medium-Range (3–5 years)

　　Build four adult enrichment class rooms.

　　Start thirty cell groups.

　　Train fifty men and women in discipleship.

Long-Range (6–10 years)

　　Hire two adult ministry interns.

　　Develop a monthly adult outreach.

　　Hire a full-time adult ministry secretary.

Facility

Short-Range (1–2 years)	*Target Date*
Complete modules and parking.	June 1
Purchase more property and develop a master plan.	June 1
Write a schedule for equipment replacement.	January 15

Medium-Range (3–5 years)

    Design a directory of rooms and buildings.

    Train maintenance team.

    Purchase additional land.

Long Range (6–10 years)

    Increase outdoor play area.

    Install perimeter fencing.

    Develop a long-range maintenance plan.

Appendix C

Pitfalls to Avoid

There are several pathological signs to look for before developing any strategy. There are also some pitfalls to avoid. The following are some of the more common problems encountered in the planning process.

Does the Organization Have a History of Resistance?

There probably is some truth to the saying "You can't teach an old dog new tricks." Rev. Bill Yeager, the former pastor of First Baptist Church in Modesto, California, became well known for his pastors conference Institute of Church Imperatives. In his strategy for change, he described the existing structure as the "carnal corral." He poured his efforts into those who were willing to grow and go. When some of the status quo saw that others were bearing fruit and wanted to as well, he grabbed them and put them to work.

Jesus seemed to have the same strategy; overlooking the religious leaders, he chose fisherman and tax collectors. One church consulting group has all but given up on breathing life into old established churches that resist change. They are putting all their efforts into church planting. Carnal resistance can be broken down, but patience and persistence is required. It is wise to determine this before accepting an appointment; one's efforts may be more fruitful elsewhere.

Being a Vehicle in a Power Struggle

Progress is determined by trust. If there are factions within the organization, change in structure or program won't help much. Internal change is needed. Healing relationships, building trust, and demonstrating love is the core of our ministry. It can't be bypassed for the sake of progress! Anyone who sweeps this under the carpet will trip over it someday. When win-lose mentalities or adversary relationships exist, spiritual renewal is the only viable alternative. If our hands are bloodied by battle like David's, we can't build the temple! Some may be called to the field of battle, but seldom will they be around to enjoy the fruits of their labor. Even Jesus had a forerunner who would call the establishment to task, but it cost John his life, "Blessed are the peacemakers: for they shall be called the children of God" (Matt. 5:9 KJV). "'Not by might nor by power, but by my Spirit,' says the LORD Almighty" (Zech. 4:6 NIV). Forcing our way is not God's way.

Is the Leadership Powerless in the Organization?

This is similar to the previous point, but the question I always ask when consulting is, "Do you have an adequate power base?" *Support* may be a better word, but if trust and confidence aren't there, how can one realistically go on? Many try intimidation, or charge others with not being submissive. This is a clear violation of 1 Peter 5:1–5, where leadership is told not to lord it over people but prove to be an example. The true basis for authority is to be found in our character and godly example, which are the only requirements for being an elder. If the credibility isn't there, then build credibility, and wait until there is enough maturity to accomplish great things for God. God will not lead us beyond our maturity. The simple truth is that no ministry will rise above its leadership base. If we want to expand our ministry, we must work at increasing the level of leadership. Adding or changing programs will not substitute for mature godly leaders. Jesus spent three years preparing leaders who would serve as the foundation for the church. This is the Lord's strategy for change: Prepare the leadership first.

Watch Out for Organizational Pathology

Find out if you are able to access information or adequate resources. Sometimes a board appoints a committee to investigate a new order, but there is no one on the committee with enough status to pull it off. Is the process legitimate, and is there commitment on the part of the policy makers? One organization had a committee that had been working toward reorganization for two years. However, there was no one on the committee that had any organizational status and they went nowhere. When I was invited to provide assistance, the first thing I did was to ask for a new committee consisting of the pastor, three critical leaders, and myself. The next thing I did was to ask how committed they were to denominational distinctives. Was there some ideology that was non-negotiable? What parameters did we have to operate in?

Do Not Unearth Too Much

It is possible to point out too many needed changes, and even the best of people become overwhelmed. People are easily discouraged, and it is never right to undermine confidence. There is an eternity of difference between "this place is really messed up, but with my help we'll make it right," and "I believe that God has begun a good work within you and by his grace we will accomplish even greater things." Paul understood this when writing to the church at Corinth, "Great is my confidence in you; great is my boasting on your behalf" (2 Cor. 7:4). There was no New Testament church more messed up than the church at Corinth; the average leader would not boast in confidence about the

Corinthian church. What Paul knew was that God is bigger than any of our perceived problems, and he was careful not to dishearten the church.

Do Not Let Diagnosis Become a Pattern of Avoidance

A prolonged diagnosis may cause others to lose heart. The one who waits until all the facts are in will wait forever. Set deadlines, and establish accountability in reporting research.

Do Not Let Diagnosis Become a Destructive Confrontation

Be aware of the negative power of confrontation. People are easily threatened and become defensive when something they are a part of is being considered for change. I learned early in the ministry the three C's of change: confrontation, conflict, and change.

Change begins with confrontation and success is usually determined in the first step. Why is change needed if there isn't something a little wrong? As Christians, we are free to grow (change) because we are loved and accepted; we don't change in order to gain God's acceptance. The same must be true in any change relationship. Also, stress the advantages of change, not the horror.

Watch Favorite Diagnosis

We all have had our fill with the "expert" who can solve all our problems if we would only do _____! People who generalize, or over simplify are a pest to the process of change. We live in a complex age and few problems are one-dimensional. One man seldom has the complete picture or the perfect perspective. The best change agent is the one who knows the right resources, can draw the people together, and help them come to common objectives. People are committed to objectives they believe are their own.

Avoid Fire Fighting

Do not always look at what appears immediate and important; there may be much larger hidden issues. I have learned in counseling that the presenting problem is seldom the real issue. Working through the symptoms to the core is a unique skill.

Ask some key questions first:

- Is there a mission statement?
- Are there any present goals or objectives?
- Is there an adequate structure to achieve those goals?
- Is there communication up and down in the organization?
- Are there sufficient resources available?
- What is the reward system and is there sufficient motivation?

Murphy's Law

This axiom states that if anything can go wrong, it will. Murphy's Law situations are basically out of your control. When it comes, you have two choices: fight it or face it. If you try to fight it, you will be hitting your head on a proverbial stonewall. The best option is to face reality and respond positively. Accept that you cannot change it, and then work to find a solution to the problem.

Here are some ideas to keep in mind:

- Remember who called you. God is bigger than what is wrong.
- Keep focused on the vision God has given you.
- Keep the main thing the main thing.
- Be a problem solver and not a part of the problem.
- Use failure as stepping stones to future success.
- Remember: It is always darkest before the morning; never give up hope.

- Do what you can with what you have where you are; remembering the promise that God will give the increase (1 Cor. 3:6).
- Make up your mind that no matter what happens, you will be a lover of people. Love people regardless of how they treat you. You will always win with love.[1]

NOTE

1. Adapted from Dale E. Galloway, "Look Out for Murphy's Law," *Net Results* (May 1997): 18–19.

Resources

Bryson, John M. *Strategic Planning for Public and Nonprofit Organizations*. San Francisco: John Wiley & Sons, Inc., 2004.

Callahan, Kennon L. *Twelve Keys to an Effective Church: Strategic Planning for Mission*. San Francisco: Harper & Row, 1983, 2005.

Kaye, Jude. *Strategic Planning for Nonprofit Organizations*. San Francisco: John Wiley & Sons, Inc., 2005.

Kloop, Henry. *The Ministry Playbook: Strategic Planning for Effective Churches*. Grand Rapids, Mich.: Baker Books, 2005.

Malphurs, Aubrey. *Advanced Strategic Planning*. Grand Rapids, Mich.: Baker Books, 2005.

———. *Developing a Vision for Ministry in the 21st Century*. Grand Rapids, Mich.: Baker Books, 2007.

———. *Values Driven Leadership*. Grand Rapids, Mich.: Baker Books, 2006.

Mancini, Will. *Church Unique: How Missional Leaders Cast Vision, Capture Culture, and Create Movement*. San Francisco: Jossey-Bass, 2008.

Migliore, R. Henry. *Church and Ministry Strategic Planning*. Binghamton, N.Y.: The Haworth Press, Inc. 1994.

Wren, Bud. *Innovative Planning: Your Church in 4-D*. Atlanta: Chalice Press, 2008.

About the Author

Gary L. McIntosh, D.Min., Ph.D., is an internationally known author, speaker, consultant, and professor of Christian Ministry and Leadership at Talbot School of Theology, Biola University located in La Mirada, California. He has written extensively in the field of pastoral ministry, leadership, generational studies, and church growth.

Dr. McIntosh received his BA from Colorado Christian University in Biblical Studies, an M.Div. from Western Conservative Baptist Seminary in Pastoral Studies, a D.Min. from Fuller Theological Seminary in Church Growth Studies, and a Ph.D. from Fuller Theological Seminary in Intercultural Studies.

As president of the McIntosh Church Growth Network, a church consulting firm he founded in 1989, Dr. McIntosh has served over five thousand churches in eighty-three denominations throughout the United States and Canada. As the 1995 and 1996 president of the American Society for Church Growth, he edited the *Journal of the American Society for Church Growth* for fourteen years. He currently edits *Growth Points*, a nationally read newsletter offering insights for ministry leaders in the United States and Canada.

Presentations and Workshops

Gary L. McIntosh speaks to numerous churches, nonprofit organizations, schools, and conventions each year. Services available include keynote presentations, seminars and workshops, training courses, and ongoing consultation.

For a live presentation of the material found in *Here Today, There Tomorrow* or to request a catalog of materials or other information on Dr. McIntosh's availability and ministry, contact:

McIntosh Church Growth Network
PO Box 892589
Temecula, CA 92589-2589
951-506-3086
www.churchgrowthnetwork.com